50 R.E. Lessons from Bible World

*To Kathleen and Audrey,
and to Jan: thank you.*

A complete guide
for teachers

50 R.E. LESSONS
FROM
BIBLE WORLD

Diane Walker

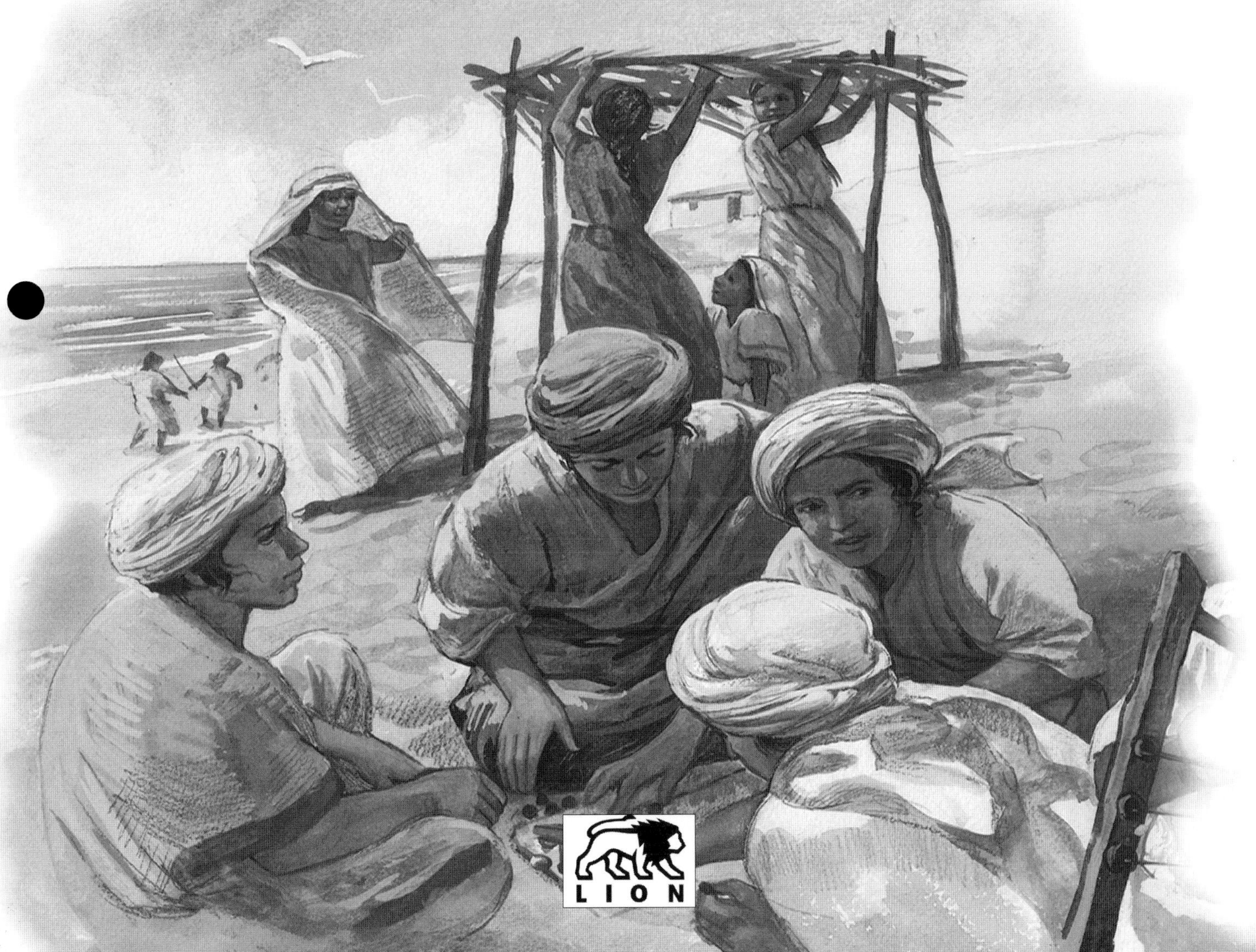

Text copyright © 1999 Diane Walker
Illustrations on pp. 15, 25, 28, 29, 33, 35, 37, 41, 44, 50, 52, 53,
57, 58, 62, 63, 69, 80, 95, 99, 100, 105, 107, 108 and 120
copyright © 1999 Ian Mitchell
This edition copyright © 1999 Lion Publishing

The author asserts the moral right
to be identified as the author of this work

Published by
Lion Publishing plc
Sandy Lane West, Oxford, England
www.lion-publishing.co.uk
ISBN 0 7459 3818 3

First edition 1999
10 9 8 7 6 5 4 3 2 1 0

All rights reserved

A catalogue record for this book is available
from the British Library

Typeset in 10/12 Humanist521
Printed and bound in Britain

Acknowledgments
The author gratefully acknowledges the support of Margaret
Cooling in the preparation of this manuscript. Her advice and
encouragement have been, as ever, vital and valued. I would also
like to thank my husband Robin for his technical and moral
support. Neither should the patience and understanding of my
daughters be unacknowledged. I am indebted to Jon Webster for
allowing me to use one of his sketches in this book. Final
responsibility for any errors rests, of course, with the author alone.

Palm cross illustrations on p. 83 from *The Easter Activity Book*,
published by Lion Publishing.

Illustrations by Chris Molan on pp. 3, 16, 40, 89, 91, 93 from *Bible
World* series, copyright © Lion Publishing.

Illustration on p. 85 by Studio Simone Boni/Studio Luigi Galante
taken from *Settlers, Warriors and Kings* (*Bible World* series, volume
2), published by Lion Publishing.

Contents

Introduction 7

God

Making things
God the Creator 10

Keeping a promise
God is trustworthy: the Flood 12

... and back again!
God is in control: Joseph (2) 14

Escape from Egypt
God the rescuer and provider: Moses 16

How to live
God the lawgiver: the Ten Commandments 18

God and people
Two-way promises!: covenants 21

The two mountains
God is powerful and gentle: Elijah 22

Going fishing!
God is merciful: Jonah 23

Titles and names of God 24

God's friends

When things go wrong
Disobeying God: the Fall 28

Leaving home to go home!
Obeying God: Abraham 30

What's in a name?
God's friends are not perfect: Jacob and Esau 32

From riches to rags...
God's friends are not perfect: Joseph (1) 34

'Trust me!'
Trusting God: Joshua 36

Impossible jobs!
Trusting God is not always easy: the Judges 38

Caring
Caring for each other: Ruth 41

A child and a king
God's surprising choice of friends:
Samuel and Saul 43

A champion!
God's friends are helped: David and Goliath 46

Wise—and foolish!
God's friends are not perfect: Solomon 48

Far from home
When things go wrong:
in exile and the three friends 50

The brave queen
God's friends face difficult choices: Esther 52

Jesus' life

Preparing for Jesus
John the Baptist 56

Baby in a stable
Jesus' birth 58

Part of a team!
Jesus' baptism 62

The wrong thing to do!
Jesus' temptation 64

Jesus' team
The disciples 65

It's a miracle!
Jesus' miracles 67

Jesus' checklist
People Jesus met 71

Jesus the teacher
Jesus' teaching 74

Jesus' stories
The Parables 79

Jesus the King
Entry into Jerusalem 82

Jesus' anger The Temple	84
A special meal The Last Supper	86
In the garden Prayer, arrest and Judas	88
The end? The death of Jesus	90
The great surprise! The Resurrection (1)	92
Failure and forgiveness The Resurrection (2)	94
'See you again!' The Ascension	96

The Holy Spirit

The church's birthday Pentecost	98
Jesus' teaching about the Holy Spirit Spiritual gifts	100
The Helper The Holy Spirit	102

Early church

Growth—and a death The early church and Stephen	104
Success and failure Peter's life	106
An enemy who became a friend Paul	108
The travelling teacher Paul's missionary journeys	110
Others helped too Some other important people in Acts	113

The Bible

A book of books	116
Other suggested topics	123
Chronological index	124
People index	124
Thematic index	125
Appendix	127

Introduction

This book is intended to be used in parallel with the books of the *Bible World* series. It contains lesson plans based upon the use of these books, and refers closely to them. The material is intended to be as flexible as possible, with alternative approaches and activities presented throughout. It is hoped that it will enable teachers to make effective use of the wealth of information contained in the series, and will facilitate pupils' use of the books. (For easy reference, the left- and right-hand pages of a spread in the *Bible World* books are referred to as 'a' and 'b'—4.12.a, for example, refers to book 4, spread 12, left-hand page.)

The lessons are divided into several sections. The order of these varies within the lessons, but the usual pattern is given below:

1. Introduction

This section introduces the theme of the lesson to the pupils, firmly anchoring it in their own experience.

2. Biblical or core material

This centres on the theme to be explored in the lesson, citing and using the material in the books. Reference is also made sometimes to supporting or additional material in the Bible.

3. Activities

There are usually two activities. These encourage further thought about and exploration of the theme by the pupils themselves. Class activities may feature here. Alternative activities are usually given for *younger* and *older pupils*, although, obviously, teachers can use ability as a guiding factor here, as well as age. A 'further' activity follows in the majority of lessons, containing an activity which is usually self-directed further exploration of the theme under consideration. (This can be used as an Extension exercise.)

4. Assembly suggestion/s

These are suggestions only. They offer ways of utilizing work done by the pupils during the lessons.

5. Think about it

Some lessons contain this section, encouraging private thought about an aspect of the lesson. It should be stressed that the pupils are under no obligation to share their thoughts.

6. Cross-references

It is possible to find further information in the books about virtually any subject. The index volume—the *Bible World Factfinder*—and the books' own indices make cross-referencing easy. This section does not appear in every lesson, is not exhaustive, and merely suggests some passages which are particularly helpful, with the intention of showing the pupils how such cross-referencing can help them in their own work.

Each lesson belongs in a particular group, which indicates the main theme of topic contained in the lesson. These have been chosen to include topics mentioned in the majority of county syllabi. Each lesson also has a number of underlined topics or themes at its beginning. These are intended to indicate some other themes under which the lesson could be studied. This is not an exhaustive list, but should help teachers to tie in the material with their own syllabi.

Indices

There is a contents page at the beginning of the book. This gives a story's title; its subtitle, which relates to the title of the section; and also the title by which the biblical episode on which it is based is generally known. At the end of the book, there are three indices, designed to help the teacher to find any subject or person contained in the book quickly and easily. These are:

1. Thematic index: this brings together the themes mentioned at the beginning of each lesson, enabling

teachers to trace a topic throughout the book.

2. Chronological index: this has been included for teachers who wish to adopt a chronological approach to the Bible and its stories, and to show where a particular story fits into the overall structure and history of the Bible.

3. People index: this is to enable teachers to locate stories about particular characters quickly and easily.

Presentation

When presenting this material, care should always be taken to ground the beliefs referred to therein in the Christian faith community. Statements of belief should be prefaced with phrases such as, 'Christians believe that…', 'To Christians, this was important because…' The pupils' agreement with any statement should not be assumed, so that their integrity is respected and preserved. When activities ask for a statement of belief—as in the work on God—phrases such as 'Christians believe that…' are suggested as a means of distancing the belief statement from the pupils.

Sensitivity is also needed particularly when dealing with such issues as the character of God. There are suggestions in the relevant section about distancing the work for pupils who have negative experiences of authority figures, especially in the home.

Some lessons contain alternative approaches and/or material: the 'Bible' and Christmas sections, for instance, are designed to offer teachers the chance to select suitable material for whatever length of time they have available for the subject, giving the opportunity of revisiting the subject matter at another time. Similarly, the second activity usually, but not exclusively, is not dependent on the first, so that teachers can choose either, depending on a number of factors, such as time available.

Health and safety

The usual health and safety regulations must be referred to and followed when practical activities are suggested.

God

Making things

Creation

Caring for the environment

God the Creator

You will need

- items made by the pupils
- card and felt-tips for making labels.

Preparation

Ask pupils to bring in things they have made, for a display; or use things made in the classroom.

Introduction

Talk about the display of things the pupils have made. Keeping the discussion positive and not destructive, ask the pupils if they are pleased with their own work. Which parts/aspects of their work please them especially? (Allow the pupils to comment only on their own work.) If they repeated the piece of work, would they change anything about it? Would they use different methods? Do they think that they could improve their work?

Biblical or core material

The first book of the Bible tells the Jewish and Christian story of creation. It tells how God created the world, and it tells us what God thought of everything in it.

Read 1.2.a.

Ask the children what the story says about God's opinion of creation. Emphasize that God was pleased with everything: no second 'go' was needed, because everything was as good as it could be the first time.

Activity 1

Make a display of things God created to go alongside the display of the pupils' work. Some articles—such as flowers—can be used. Other items can be represented by pictures—drawn or cut out. Make a title for each display, describing what the display is and saying who made the things in it (e.g. 'Class 2 made the things in this display.' or 'The Bible says that God made all of these things.'). According to the Bible, what would God have said about each created thing? Ask the pupils to make labels for these things, reading, 'God said, "I am very pleased with this… It is very good." '

Tell the pupils that they need to label the individual parts of their display now. What do they need to tell others about their work? (Bring out the need for the maker's name, description/title of object.) Is there anything else they want people to know? Are any of the things fragile? How should they be handled? Can they suggest and make labels which will tell other people how to handle their work? How would they feel if they asked another class to look after their work, and the pupils in that class were careless and broke it? What if they gave their own piece of work to someone in their family, and they broke it?

Look at the display of all the things God made. God asked some people to look after these things.

Read 1.2.b.

Whom did God ask to look after the world? God made men and women stewards of the earth: this means that they were its caretakers—they were to take care of it. Do they think that humans have done this, or have they been careless in the way they have treated the earth? Discuss some of the things humans have done that have spoiled the earth and its animals and plants.

Activity 2

If God could have labelled everything created, what would the labels have said? Make labels for the display of God's work.

Think about it

God did not need to make these labels for creation because the job of looking after it had been given to humans. What went wrong?

Activity 3

Think about the damage people have done to the earth and its animals. Read the story of creation again. List some of the things God made. Don't just put 'plants'; think about a plant you particularly like. Do the same for birds, sea and land animals, trees, a river or sea, a country, etc. Write a poem with this framework, altering the words as necessary:

God made the pine tree,
Saw that it was good.
People dug up the pine tree,
Made a road instead.

The class can work on this individually, or communally, to produce a class display.

Further

1. Many ancient civilizations have their own creation stories. Read those on 10.5.a & b. How are these different from the Jewish and Christian account? How is the God of the biblical account different from the other gods mentioned?

2. What can we do about the damage that is being done to the earth? Find out about a local, national or international campaign or society that is trying to end or repair this damage. (For example: local wildlife groups would be helpful here, with information about local projects and sites. See the 'Useful addresses' section at the back of this book for the address of Friends of the Earth and of the Young Ornithologists' Club.)

Assembly suggestion

Talk about the value of made things and the need to look after them. Show some examples from pupils' work, labelled with 'Fragile! Handle with care!' Talk about the Christian belief that God appointed people as stewards or caretakers of the earth. Show examples or pictures of creation. Label them similarly.

Keeping a promise

Promises

Trust

God is trustworthy: the Flood

Preparation

Activity 1, with the 'promise cards', could be done a week in advance—so the pupils have already experienced how hard it can be to keep a promise.

You will need

- pieces of card for the pupils
- a banknote (a magnifying glass would be useful for this).

Introduction

Show the children the banknote. Ask them what it is worth. Point out that it is really worthless—just a piece of paper. But if you took it into a shop, you could buy something (name something appropriate for the note you are using) with it. What makes it worth anything is some of the writing on it. Pass it round (with the magnifying glass, if you have one) and let each pupil find and read or look at the words 'I promise to pay the bearer on demand the sum of…' and the signature of the Chief Cashier. Explain who has signed it, and then explain how banknotes originated and why they have these words on and what they mean. Ask them: 'If people did not believe the Bank of England would keep this promise, what would the note be worth?'

Activity 1

Unless one of us becomes Chief Cashier of the Bank of England, we will not have a chance to make money notes worth anything! But we can make other ordinary paper valuable in another way. Give out the pieces of card. Ask them to think about a promise they could make to someone which would please them. They could promise their mother that they would clear the table every evening for a week. They could promise their father that they would dust every evening. They could promise you that they would read their reading book every night for a week! When they have chosen a promise (make sure that they are all realistic!), ask them to write it on the card, or to draw themselves keeping that promise. Then ask them to sign it—or write their initials. They have now made their own 'promise card', like the banknote. Remind them that the note was only valuable because people trusted the bank to keep the promise made on it. Will people be able to trust them to keep their promise?

Biblical or core material

Discuss this idea of trustworthiness a little more. Why do we need to trust people? How do we feel if we cannot trust people? Think of instances where we need to trust people, and situations where people let us down—but keep it hypothetical. Point out that only the person who made the promise and the person to whom it was made will know if it has been kept. Will the pupils be trustworthy?

The Bible tells about a man and his family who risked their lives because they believed that the promises God made to them would be kept.

Read top of 1.4.a

to set the scene, and then

 Read 1.4.b about Noah.

God told Noah that he would be safe in the ark. What did Noah do as a result? Was it easy for Noah to trust God? It was a very strange thing to be asked to do, and people laughed at him. Later, it must have been terrifying to be locked up in the ark, unable to get out, and to see the grass, then the trees, then the hills and mountains disappearing. But Noah still trusted God. Noah had already learned that he could trust God. He already knew that God could look after him, loved him and wanted to keep him safe.

 Read 1.5.a & b.

Then, after the Flood, God gave Noah and all people another promise, and this time they were given something to remind them about God's trustworthiness—a rainbow. From then on, people would have a reminder of God's love.

Activity 2

 Read 1.5.b—'Did you know?'

and then answer these questions:

1. Why do you think these groups use the rainbow?

2. Design your own badge using the rainbow. This could be on a round or square piece of card, which could be turned into a badge with a safety-pin; or it could be a shaped badge.

Activity 3

Christians believe that God always keeps promises. They believe that God is trustworthy. Make a 'promise card' from God. Find out what colours are in a rainbow. Draw and colour a rainbow on a piece of card, and along its edge write the promise God gave to Noah:

'Never again will a flood destroy the earth.'

Further

There are other accounts of great floods from other civilizations.

 Read 1.5—'Other flood stories'.

What differences can you find between these and the biblical account about the causes of the Flood? Is there any difference between God and the gods in the other accounts?

Assembly suggestion

Talk about the promise on banknotes: trustworthiness makes them valuable. Noah believed God, and built the ark—tell his story. To Christians today, the rainbow is a sign of God's trustworthiness.

... and back again!

Forgiveness

Families

God is in control: Joseph (2)

Introduction

If necessary, remind them of Joseph's situation. Life seemed to be as bad as it could get for him. But things were about to change!

Read 1.13.a—'Joseph's rise to fame'.

How had Joseph's life changed? He was now safe—but his brothers did not want or expect any of this to happen! What did they want to happen to him?

Mini-activity

What would the pupils expect Joseph to say to his brothers now if he met them? Ask them to write this down, or to whisper it to another pupil, before you read any more of the story.

Biblical or core material

Read 1.13.a & b—'The Terrible Famine' and 'A Happy Ending'.

Joseph seemed to be acting strangely. Discuss why he did not tell them at first who he was, and why he planted the cup in Benjamin's sack. Ask the pupils to read or report what they thought he would say to his brothers. Then read this passage from the Bible: 'I am your brother Joseph. Do not be frightened, or angry with yourselves for selling me. For it was God who sent me here to save many lives—including your own.'

Were any of them close to what he really said? Why did he say this? Joseph had been treated very badly by his brothers. He had endured danger, hardship and terror—but he had realized that God had kept him safe and had used all of his experiences to carry out what God wanted to do: to keep the Israelites safe. The brothers did not know this would happen. They just wanted to get rid of Joseph. But God had been in control all the time. Joseph forgave his brothers. Do the pupils think that this was an easy thing to do?

Activity 1

Prepare for a radio interview with Joseph. As a class, decide which questions you need to ask him so that your listeners will understand what has happened. For instance, 'How did you come to be living in Egypt at all?' 'Why did you plant the cup in your own brother's sack?' Once the questions have been decided on, the pupils can each write their answers to them, or they can work in pairs to write the answers. Some can then act out their interview for the class or record it. Make sure that Joseph has a chance to include his belief that God had used the past years to save his family.

Activity 2

The pupils can work in groups to produce a board game of Joseph's life; this could be on the same lines as 'Snakes and Ladders'. They need first to list the main events in his life, and his reactions to some of them. Decide which are 'snakes' and which are 'ladders'. For instance, the brothers' jealousy became a 'snake' in Joseph's life because it led to a disastrous event. His forgiveness was a 'ladder' because it led to the rest of the family settling in safety in Egypt. Begin with his birth, and end with the arrival of Jacob in Egypt. When the games are finished, they might like to exchange them with others in the class. They can then decide which factors work well in such games. Or perhaps the games could be lent to a younger class.

Younger pupils can make a simple plate puppet. Each pupil needs one paper plate, and a circular piece of paper cut to fit the plate as shown. This has Joseph's eyes and nose drawn on it. It is attached by a brass tack, as shown, to the plate. On one edge of the plate, a smiling mouth is drawn, with a sad one opposite it. The inner circle can then be moved as the story is told. Working in pairs, the pupils can decide which are the main events in Joseph's life, and write a sentence for each one. One of them can then read this out, or tell the story from memory, while the other alters the puppet's expression appropriately to match Joseph's feelings at the time.

Assembly suggestion

The interviews can be used to tell the story of Joseph in Egypt, or the plates can be used as a narrator reads it.

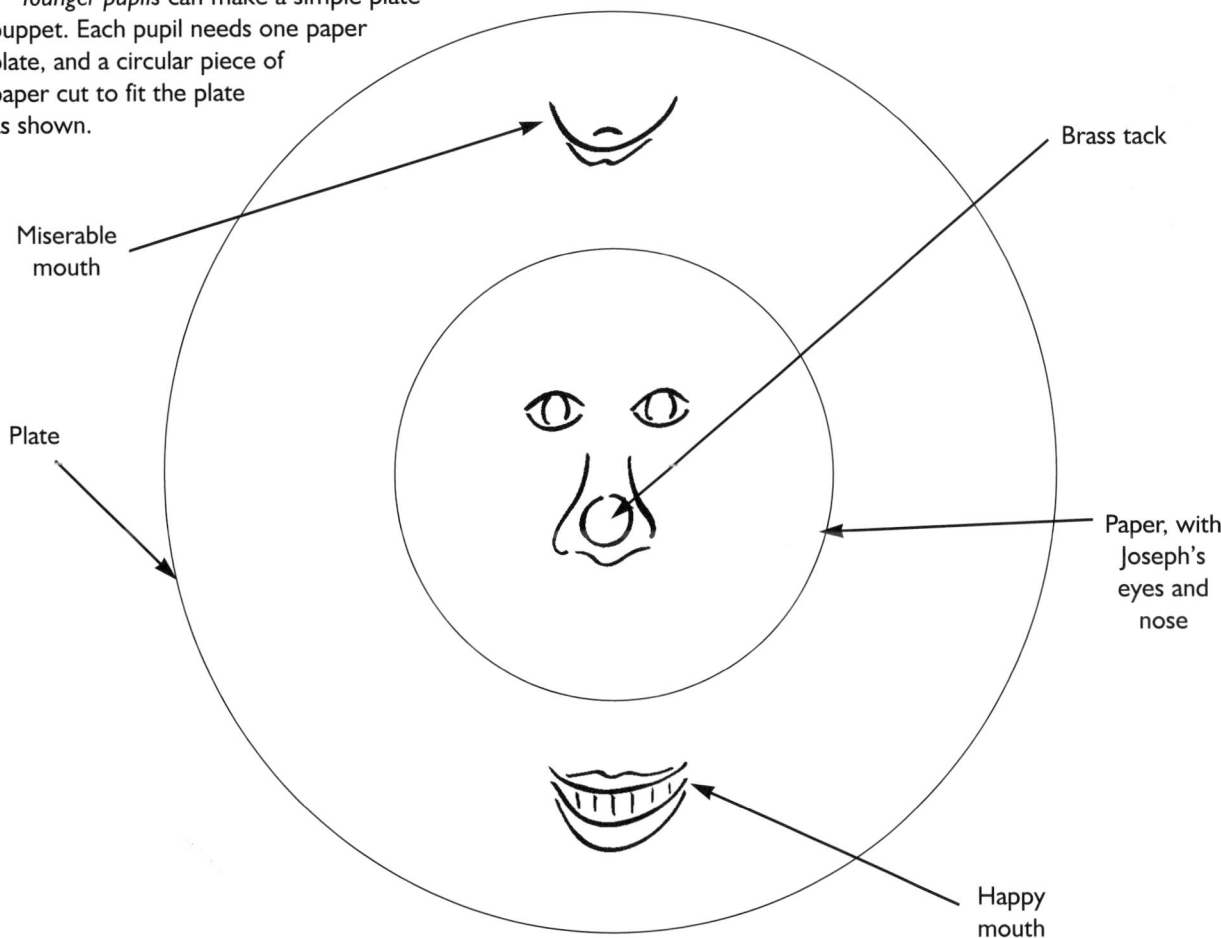

Escape from Egypt

God's care

The Passover

God the rescuer and provider: Moses

Biblical or core material

Many years after Joseph died, the Israelites were still living in Egypt. But life there had changed greatly for them.

Read 1.14.a & b.

Activity 1

Either:
1. One day, terrible things started to happen in Egypt—first of all to the Israelites and the Egyptians, and then just to the Egyptians.

Read 1.16.b—*first seven plagues only.*

Imagine that you are an Egyptian living through these things. You have heard people talking about someone called Moses. You want to find out what is happening to your country. Is it something to do with him? Find out all you can about him from 1.15.a & b, and 1.16.a. Make notes about him—for instance: who is he? Why does he keep going to see Pharaoh? Why are these things happening to us? Write up the results of your research.

Some pupils might prefer to listen as you read the passages, and then decide what are the important events of Moses' life. They can then record their information by drawing pictures of these important events.

As Egyptians, do they think that Pharaoh should let the Israelites go? They can write down the reasons for their answers. Most of the Egyptians must have been reluctant to lose their slave labour. But soon they changed their minds. Why did this happen?

📖 *Read 1.16.b and 1.17.a about the final plague, and the Passover.*

Write a final paragraph, describing their feelings as they watch the Israelites leaving and hear about their escape from their forces at the Red Sea—or they can draw Egyptian heads with thought bubbles. The pupils can then switch to being Israelites, describing or drawing the events of that last night in Egypt and the Passover, and their escape at the Red Sea.

Or:
2. Moses was an important person in the history of the Israelites. He led them out of slavery in Egypt. But who was he? What do we know about him? Form the class into research teams, and give them each a title to work on:
- Moses as a baby and child—1.15.a & b
- Why he left Egypt and his life in the desert—1.16.a 'Escape from Slavery' and 'The Flames in the Bush'
- Moses and Pharaoh—the plagues—1.16.a 'Moses meets Pharaoh' and 1.16.b 'The Plagues'
- The Passover—1.17.a 'The Passover night'
- Escape and the Red Sea—1.17.a 'A chance to escape'
- God provides food and water—1.17.a 'Free at last'
- Their life in the desert—1.18.a & b.

Each group can provide a paragraph on their subject. These can be shared, in order, either orally or as printouts from the computer.

Younger pupils could draw a picture of each section, and these can then be put together like a jigsaw on the wall to tell the whole story.

Further

Pupils can look at the celebration of the Passover in 8.8.

Assembly suggestion

Pupils can use the work they have done to tell the story of Moses, either reading their own sections, or holding up their pictures and describing them.

Cross-references

- 7.3.a & b—Egypt
- 7.17.a & b—Moses and the Promised Land.

How to live

Fairness

Telling the truth

Rules

Caring for others

Responsibility to others

God the lawgiver: the Ten Commandments

Introduction

'Rules, rules, rules—that's all I ever hear about!' Andrew shouted. ' "Don't do that!", "Do this!", "Don't walk there!", "You know you're not supposed to do that!" I've had enough! No more rules for me!'

Next day, he set off for school. It was difficult to get over the road. The school crossing man was there—but none of the car-drivers wanted to stop. He and Andrew had to keep jumping back onto the kerb. So Andrew was late for school—but no one else seemed to mind. He had missed half of the maths lesson, and he liked maths. But he couldn't work, because no one else was working. Tom was flying his model aeroplane, which didn't seem at all safe to Andrew. Sure enough, it hit Elizabeth on the head—but no one told Tom off. At break, it was even worse. Gangs of the bigger children raced round the playground, and several of Class 1 finished up in tears on the ground. But, again, no one seemed to mind what happened. Back in the classroom, it was just as noisy as before. Andrew looked for his lunch. It was an iced bun with his initial 'A' on it. Mum had made it specially—but it had gone! He saw Michael eating it. 'Miss Easton!' Andrew called. 'Michael's got my lunch!'

The teacher sighed, and put down the magazine she was reading. 'Well?' she said. 'Why shouldn't he have your lunch? Perhaps he was hungry.' Andrew was amazed. What was happening? It couldn't be right for Michael to take his lunch, could it? What was wrong with everyone today?

Discuss the story. Many rules were ignored in it, some more obvious than others! What areas of life did they cover? Why were these rules needed to govern these areas? What were the results of having/not having the rules? What other areas of life need rules? Why do they need them? Imagine life in these areas without the rules.

Activity 1

The pupils could write about the rest of Andrew's day, bringing in the other areas of life where rules are needed. How will they end the story? What will Andrew have learned? *Younger pupils* can discuss these issues with the teacher, as the class suggests how the story could continue.

Biblical or core material

The Israelites, led by Moses, had left Egypt where they had been slaves. Now they were living out in the countryside, travelling through deserts and mountains. If they found a good place to stop, with fresh water, they would stay there for a while. They lived in tents, and had to find their own food. It was a very different life from the one they had lived in Egypt. There, they had been slaves, but their food had been provided for them, and they had never had to think about how to behave. They were slaves—and this meant that they did as they were told. Now, out here, they had no rules to live by. They needed to know how to treat other people and how God wanted them to behave. When they reached their new land, they would need rules about how to live, too. So God gave them a set of rules.

Read 1.19.a & b—'Did you know?'

Discuss the two types of rules the Ten Commandments can be divided into. Discuss with the children whether this set of rules would cover all the areas of the Israelites' life. Refer to the two sentences (from Leviticus and Deuteronomy) which summed up the Law: 'Love the Lord with all your heart and with all your soul and with all your strength' and 'Love your neighbour as you love yourself'. Help pupils to relate these to the two parts of the Ten Commandments.

As well as these basic ten laws, God also gave them many other laws to help them understand how to follow the Ten Commandments. These laws or rules interpreted the Ten Commandments, showing the people how to work them out in their everyday lives. For instance, the eighth commandment says, 'Do not steal', and Leviticus 6:1–7 lists these different ways in which someone might steal from someone else: using something they have been asked to look after, cheating, keeping lost property. God wanted these rules to help people keep the commandments. If they did their best to obey the rules, then they could be sure that they were in no danger of breaking the commandments.

Activity 2

There is an old Jewish saying that the smaller rules were 'a hedge' around the Ten Commandments. This means that the smaller rules were to protect the greater rules—the Ten Commandments. They were to keep the people away from any danger of breaking the Ten Commandments. If they were keeping the lesser rules, then they could not be breaking the Ten Commandments. For the lesser rules showed them how the Ten Commandments worked out in practice, in their everyday lives. Below are some of the Ten Commandments, with a few of the lesser rules which protected each one. The pupils can choose one, and write it in the centre of the page. Then they can write the others as a continuous 'hedge' around the main commandment.

'Do not kill.'
- ■ 'When you build a new house, make it safe by building a wall around the edge of the flat roof, so that you will not be the cause of someone's death if they fall off the roof.' (Deuteronomy 22:8)
- ● 'Anyone who deliberately kills someone else is guilty of murder.' (Exodus 21:14)
- ▲ 'If someone kills someone else accidentally, they must still be punished—but not for murder.' (Exodus 21:13)
- ■ 'If a bull kills someone, and its owner knew that it was dangerous but did not keep it safely away from people, then the owner must be punished too. (Exodus 21:28–29)

'Do not steal.'
- ▲ 'Do not cheat people who are working for you just because they are poor and depend on you. Pay them fairly and on time.' (Deuteronomy 24:14–15)
- ■ 'Do not use two different sets of weights and measures, in order to cheat people. Use accurate weights and measures, for God hates it when people are dishonest.' (Deuteronomy 25:15–16)
- ▲ 'If someone injures someone else so that they cannot work, then they must pay for the time and work they have taken from them.' (Exodus 21:18–19)
- ■ 'If someone digs a pit, and a donkey or cow falls into it and dies, then that person must pay the animal's owner for the loss of the animal.' (Exodus 21:33–34)
- ■ 'If somebody's animals break through into another person's land and damage the crops, then the owner of the animals must pay for the damage.' (Exodus 22:5)
- ■ 'If someone borrows an animal and it dies or is injured, then that person must pay its owner for its loss.' (Exodus 22:14)
- ■ 'If you find your neighbour's cow, take it back to them.' (Exodus 23:4)

'Do not tell lies.'
- ● 'A person must speak up about what he or she knows when there is an enquiry.' (Leviticus 5:1)
- ▲ 'Do not spread rumours.' (Exodus 23:1)
- ▲ 'Do not help someone who has done something wrong by telling lies to protect them.' (Exodus 23:1)
- ▲ 'Do not just say what everyone else is saying if it is not the truth.' (Exodus 23:2)
- ▲ 'Do not let yourself be bribed into telling lies.' (Exodus 23:8)

Younger pupils can write out one of these Ten Commandments. Remind them that the Bible says that the Ten Commandments were originally carved into tablets or flat pieces of stone. What sort of surface or texture does stone have? Is there anything that feels like this in or around school (e.g. brick)? They can choose a suitable script on the computer, and print out a commandment. They can then do a rubbing on this paper, using wax crayon in a suitable colour for stone and placing the paper over their chosen textured surface. These can then be displayed.

Activity 3

Some of the laws above are marked with a ▲. Pupils can write out some of these, and then explain in their own words just what these mean in everyday life. Or they could write a short scene to show how these things happen—for instance, someone being forced to tell lies. Do they agree with the punishments and degree of guilt?

Younger pupils can draw someone stealing or lying. They could use a series of pictures to show why these things are wrong.

Further

There are some laws marked with a ■ in the lists above. These do not make much sense to us nowadays without a lot of explanation. The pupils can write them out, and then think of modern versions of them which would carry the same meaning. They will have to think carefully about what each law is actually saying.

Assembly suggestion

- Pupils could present some of the outdated laws and explain what they mean in modern terms. They could act these out.
- They could use their own stories to explore why we need rules.
- They could read out two or three of the commandments, and then explain some of the meanings of them that they have been looking at.

Cross-references

- Weights and measures—9.14.b
- Laws—9.2.a, 3.a, 4.a & b.

The box made to hold the tablets on which God's Law was written was a portable wooden chest overlaid with gold.

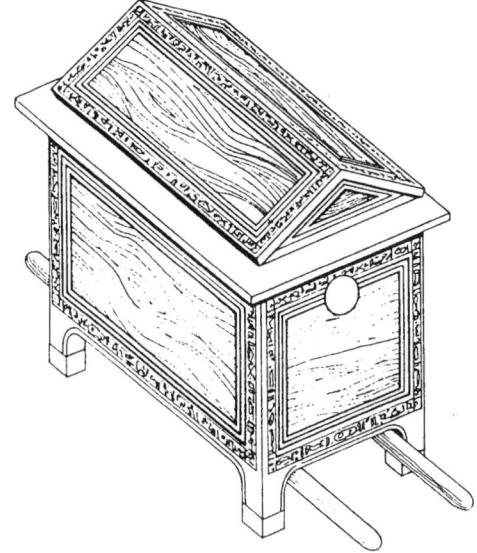

God and people

Promises

Trusting

Two-way promises!: covenants

Introduction

A covenant is an agreement between two people or two groups of people. They both agree to keep certain promises, and to do certain things. A marriage is a covenant between two people. It is the giving and receiving of vows or promises. Discuss with the pupils some of the promises that are exchanged during the service.

Activity 1

The pupils can write a 'Covenant between New Friends'. Discuss what sort of things could be included. How could they make their list look as special and important as it could be between two people?

Biblical or core material

God made a covenant like this with the people of Israel.

Read 1.20.a—'Making a covenant' (first and last paragraphs).

This covenant could be summed up like this:
- God promised to look after the people of Israel and to give them their own land.
- The people of Israel promised to obey God's laws and to live as God wanted them to live.
- Christians believe that God never broke the covenant promises; but the people of Israel often did, and this led to many times of trouble for them.

Activity 2

Write out the promises that God and the people of Israel made to each other. It was not a covenant between two equal parties! What did the Israelites gain from it?

NOTE: the agreement or covenant between God and the Israelites was a very important event in their history. It showed them that they were God's chosen people, with special responsibilities and privileges.

Assembly suggestion

Explain the meaning of covenant. Read out their friendship covenants, stressing that they are two-way promises. Talk about God's covenant with the people, and what each side promised.

The two mountains

God's power
_____

God's justice
_____

God is powerful and gentle: Elijah

NOTE: if this is used after the lesson on Solomon, an introduction about the intervening history of the people of Israel will be needed.

Read 3.1.b and 3.2.a.

Introduction

(Adapt according to whether the lesson on names of God has been covered or not; see page 24.)

We have looked at some of the names given to God, which help us to understand more about God's character. The stories in the Bible all teach us more about God. The stories about the life of one of God's prophets—Elijah—show how this works.

Activity 1

Read 3.2.b, the section on prophets.

Make sure the pupils understand the prophet's job. Introduce Elijah and

Read 3.2.b, 3.3.a & b and 3.4.a & b.

Explain that the class is going to compose a fact file on God, using the various parts of Elijah's story. The headings are:
- God looks after people—3.2.a—'Elijah and the drought'
- God is powerful—3.3.a & b
- God understands people—3.4.a
- God is a God of justice—3.4.a.

Make sure that they understand the meaning of these.

Either:
1. Work through the four sections with the class, reading, and then asking how this shows what God is like. The pupils can record their findings under the headings, writing an account of the story, followed by a sentence showing what this shows about God.

Or:
2. Divide the pupils into groups, each taking one aspect to research and record. Their findings can then be shared with the rest of the class. With *younger pupils*, the section on 'God is a God of justice' should be omitted, and an illustration or strip cartoon of their chosen story could be drawn.

Further

Elijah's job was handed down to Elisha. There is information about him on 3.5.a & b. Read this and decide what it shows us about God.

Assembly suggestion

Present the pupils' fact file about God (omitting the 'God of justice' as necessary), and tell the stories associated with each section.

Going fishing!

Responsibility to others

Setting an example

God is merciful: Jonah

Introduction

The book of Proverbs in the Bible is a collection of wise sayings. One of them is, 'Do not gloat when your enemy is in trouble. Do not let yourself feel glad when things go wrong for him.' (Proverbs 24:17) What does 'gloat' mean? Discuss the meaning of the saying with the pupils. It is very easy to feel pleased when someone who has been unkind to us is in trouble themselves. It is easy to think, 'Well, she deserved it!'

Biblical or core material

Some of the Jews felt like this when they had come back to Jerusalem after the long years they had spent in exile. They thought, 'We are special. God has chosen us. We do not need to have anything to do with other people at all. We are better than they are.' When they heard that others were in trouble, they thought, 'Well, they deserve it!' One of the people who thought like this was a prophet called Jonah. But God showed him that God's own message for everyone was very different.

 Read 3.19.b.

What did Jonah want to do when he heard about Nineveh? Why did he feel like this? These people were his enemies, remember. What do they think God was telling Jonah about God's character? Bring out that God wanted to help and forgive everyone—not just God's special people, the Jews.

The trouble was that the Jews had only remembered part of the past. They had been chosen as God's special people. But they were chosen to do a job. They were to show others how God wanted people to live by obeying God's laws. They were to show others how loving God was by the way they treated other people. They only remembered that other people had not been chosen!

Activity 1

Christians believe that they should live in such a way that other people learn about God through them. Jesus said that Christians should be like light. A light shows us where to go on a dark night. It makes us feel safer and it shows up any danger. How can Christians be like light? Discuss the various uses/properties of light with the pupils, and for each explore how a person could be like this in life. Pupils can then write a short story or sketch to illustrate someone being like light in one of these ways. *Younger pupils* can illustrate the light being used to show the way for someone, or to protect them. They can then also draw someone helping others in one of these two ways. Some might like to design a person as a torch or lightbulb to show this.

Activity 2

Pupils can write a 'wild diary' of incredible events. For instance, they could begin: 'Yesterday, I caught a dragon…' Then they can write Jonah's 'wild diary', which will sound equally incredible! *Younger pupils* could try just Jonah's diary, after discussing the events they will need to include.

Further

Some pupils might like to see what had been happening in the years after the Exile.

 Read 3.17 and 3.18.

Assembly suggestion

Talk about being an example—good or bad—to other people. The Israelites were meant to be good examples, but often failed. Tell the story of Jonah and his opinions of other people.

Titles and names of God

Character of God

Introduction

Tell the pupils you need to write a profile of yourself. Begin to describe yourself in as many ways as possible. For instance, a teacher might be described like this:
- Mrs Brown is a mother.
- She is a sister.
- She is a wife.
- She is a cousin.
- She plays tennis.
- She is a teacher.
- She is patient.

Perhaps the pupils could contribute some lines when they see what you are doing. Point out that each of these things is true and each would tell a newcomer what you are like. But none of them would tell them everything about you. They need to know all the facts about you.

Biblical or core material

Thinking about what God is like is similar to this. We hear one story and think, 'Right, that shows us that God is loving'—or 'God loves justice'. But each of these stories only shows us a small part of God's character. As people hear more stories, they gradually build up a picture of what God is like. But Christians believe that God is so great and so different from them, that they can only think about some aspects at a time.

Several of the Bible stories used in these lessons tell us something about God. For instance, the stories about the life of Elijah show us that God is powerful and a God of justice, but is also loving and caring. So the stories in the Bible are one of the ways we can know about God.

Another way is by looking at what Jesus said about God. (See the lesson 'Jesus the teacher' on page 74.) Jesus also said that anyone who had seen him had also seen God.

Read 10.7.b.—'Jesus'.

The Bible also uses some word-pictures to help people to understand what God is like. Here are some of them:
- Love (10.6.b)
- Party-giver (10.7.a)
- Rock (10.7.b; Psalm 18:2)
- Mother-bird (10.7.b)
- Shield (Psalm 18:2; Psalm 3:3)
- Defender (Proverbs 23:10, 11)
- Shepherd (Psalm 23)
- Fortress (Psalm 18:2)
- Sun (Psalm 84:11)
- Mother (Isaiah 66:13).

Activity 1

Look up and read the passages above which give word-pictures of God. Think about how each picture would make a Christian feel. For instance, a Christian would feel warm and safe when they thought about God as being like a mother hen gathering her chicks beneath her protecting feathers. Make a wall-display of these word-pictures. For each one, draw the picture—for instance, the hen—and then write a sentence underneath beginning, 'Christians believe God is like a… because…'

Activity 2

As a class, work on a version of a word and picture wheel large enough to display on the wall and in assembly. Write the words used to describe God on the inner circle, and draw pictures to represent these words around the outer circle but in a different order. On the reverse, explanatory pictures or writing can be used to explain the meaning of the image to Christians. This can be used to explain the imagery used to other people when the pictures and words are matched up.

Further

Use the books to find out more about Christians' beliefs about God. Book 10 would be especially useful.

Assembly suggestion

Use the word and picture wheel to present some of the images used to describe God. Volunteers from other classes could choose a pair to match up, and the meaning behind that image could then be explained.

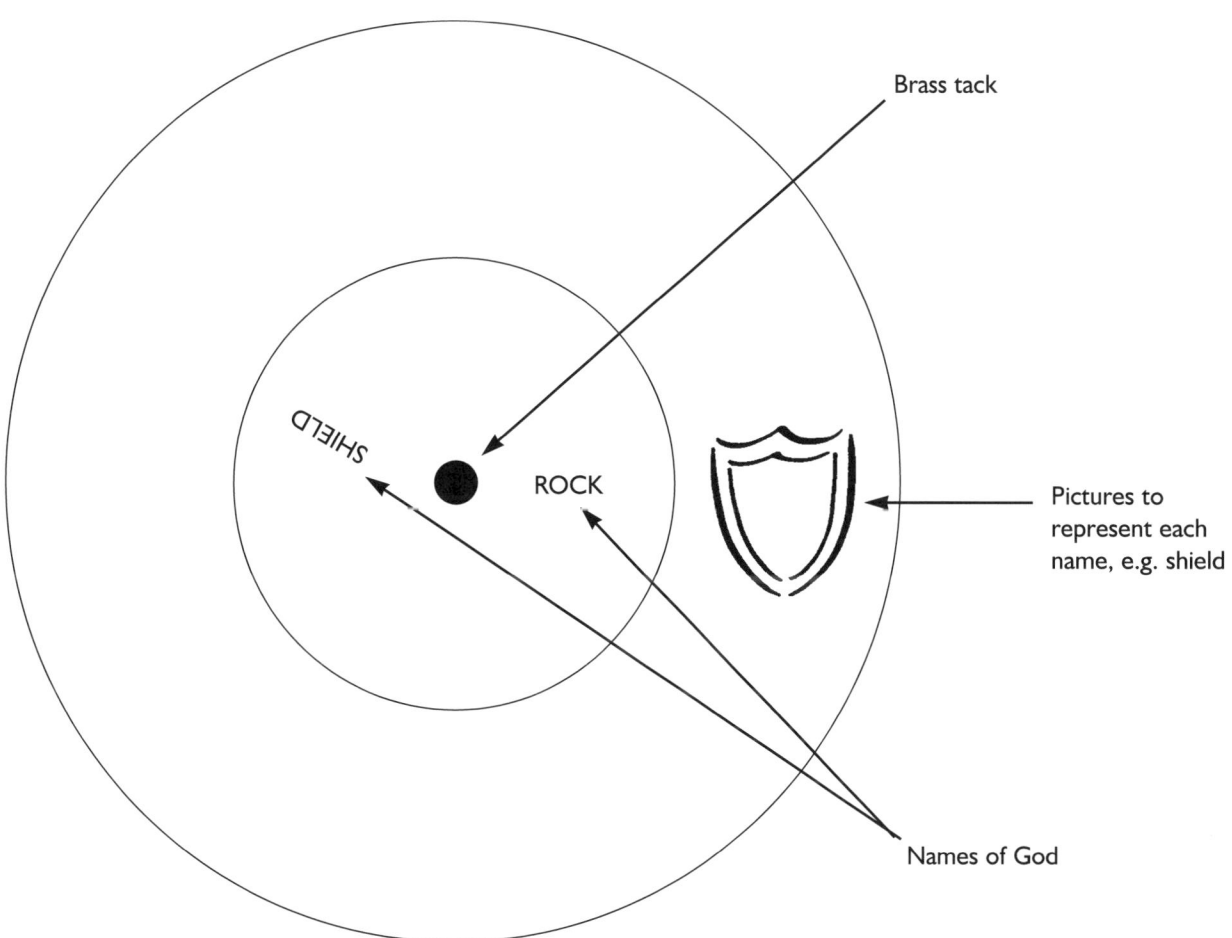

God's friends

When things go wrong

Obedience

Free will

Choices

Disobeying God: the Fall

NOTE: the story of the Fall is interpreted in many different ways by Christians. For instance, some see it as a literal account of what happened, others as a figurative interpretation of humanity's disobedience.

Introduction

Christians believe that God created a good world, a world where no person and no animal was in danger. There was no fighting, and nothing damaged the plants and trees. There was enough to eat for everyone and everything that God had created. When we think about the world today, it is easy to see that it has changed. Many people live in fear and danger, animals and plants are being destroyed all the time, and many people are short of food. What went wrong?

Biblical or core material

The Bible tells a story to show how things began to change. It tells about the first people on earth.

Read 1.3.a & b (not 'The jealous brother').

People argue a lot about this story! They wonder if there really was a garden called the Garden of Eden—and, if there was, they wonder where it was. They wonder if there really were two people who were the first people on earth, called Adam and Eve, and whether they really did eat some fruit. (And they wonder who or what the snake was.) Or, they say, is the whole story like a picture, to try to explain what happened?

Whether they believe the story is literally true or not, Christians agree that the story shows how humans turned away from God. It is like a picture of what happens when people disobey God, and decide to do just what they want instead. The fruit itself was not special or magic. But Adam and Eve disobeyed God when they ate it. That was what they did wrong—disobeying God, not just eating the fruit. As soon as Adam and Eve disobeyed God, the friendship they had shared had been damaged. Once that friendship was damaged, and they were disobeying God, they and other humans began to do other wrong things as well: they treated each other unfairly and misused God's creation. (Christians believe that the snake was Satan or evil.)

Activity 1

But why did God let all of this happen? Why didn't God make Adam and Eve remain as friends? Divide the class into pairs, but avoid the usual pairings as much as possible (or threes, to avoid an odd one out). Choose one from each pair to be a robot. The other pupil has to give the robot orders. Stress that the robots have to obey, so they must not be allowed to do anything that is dangerous or embarrassing. The pupils giving the orders must only tell them to do things that they would be willing to do themselves if you were to reverse the roles. If space is a problem, the orders can all involve only drawing or writing. When the robots have obeyed four orders, give the 'orderers' one final command to pass on: the robots are to say, ' I promise to play with you and no one else for the next week.' Then end the role play. Ask the robots how they felt. Was it pleasant to be ordered around? Did they enjoy being told with whom they had to play? Say that that order is now cancelled. What about the other pupils: how did they feel? Did any of the pupils feel that this was a good way to make friends with other people? Is this how friends would behave?

Biblical or core material

God could have ordered people to obey; God could have made them do whatever they were ordered to do. But would God and people have been friends then? Discuss. God wanted to be friends with men and women—that is why they were made. But if they *had* to obey, would God have enjoyed seeing them do as they were ordered? Why do our friends and family try to please us? Bring out the difference between doing something because we love someone, and doing something because we have to. Christians believe that God wants people to choose to live as God's friends: they are not forced to do so. Adam and Eve chose not to be friends with God in the story, and everything began to go wrong from then on.

Activity 2

When Adam and Eve ate the fruit, it was like a picture of people disobeying God. There was nothing special about the fruit. But they had been told not to eat it. Ask the class to draw and cut out as many different kinds of fruit as they can. They can look them up in appropriate books, and decide in groups who is drawing what, or you can give them the names of fruit, and tell them where to find pictures of it. At the same time, some of the pupils can be drawing and cutting out a 'branch' for the fruit to be growing on. This can be fixed on the wall. Once the fruits are ready, write 'disobedience' on one of them and tape it to the branch. Explain that this was what Adam and Eve did wrong—they disobeyed God.

Discuss with the pupils other things that people do wrong that spoil life for other people, or that spoil the earth and nature (e.g. lying, theft, greed). Ask them to write or illustrate these things on the fruit, and then tape them to the branch to form a display. Emphasize that it doesn't matter what fruit is used. The thing that is wrong—that does the damage—is what they are drawing or writing on the fruit.

Further

Pupils can work on producing leaves for a tree that would grow 'good' fruit—things that would help other people and the earth instead of harming them. For instance, one leaf could be 'caring'. Or can they think of some other way of presenting such a display?

Assembly suggestion

Pupils can re-enact the robot role-play, explaining to the others how this makes them feel, and going on to talk about free will, and what this meant in the story of Adam and Eve.

Leaving home to go home!

Perseverance

Trust

Obedience

Promises

Obeying God: Abraham

Introduction

Have any of the pupils experienced moving house lately? (Be sensitive to reasons for any move.) Ask them all to imagine that they are going to move—but not just to another house. They are going to another country: which one would they like to live in? But the country they are to move to is not the same as this one: it has no electricity, no piped water, no motorized transport—in fact, there will be no homes ready for them! Discuss the differences all of this will make to their standard of living. What will they miss about this country and their homes here? Tell them that they will not be coming back here. What will they have to take with them? What about their pets? What will they live in? How will they earn a living/feed themselves? Do they still want to go? What would make them still willing to go? What if someone promised them riches, friends and land in the new country? Would they go then? What if they did move, but had still not received anything several years afterwards, and were still struggling to live from day to day? Would they still believe that they were going to receive riches, friends and land?

Biblical or core material

There is a story in the Bible about a man who did just this: he left his own country and travelled with his family and all he owned to a strange land—just because he had been promised a land of his own and children of his own. The land he left was not the same as ours: we would think his home was primitive and badly equipped, but it was one of the best places to live at the time! He was called Abraham.

Read 1.7.a & b. Then read 1.8.b.

Abraham's new life was very different from his old life. Discuss these differences. Why did he leave Ur at all? For many years, he lived as a nomad. But he still believed in God's promises. During these years, God repeated the promises, and added to them. God promised, 'I will make you into a great nation'; 'I will give you all the land you can see'; 'You will have as many descendants as there are grains of dust'. Finally, Abraham saw one of them begin to come true. After many years, his wife, Sarah, had a son. They called him Isaac. He was the beginning of the great family God had promised to Abraham.

But what about the other promise—that he would have a new land? They were still living on other people's land, having to ask permission to stay there. It was many more years before his descendants began to take over Canaan.

Activity 1

Could you have believed in some promises for as long as Abraham did, living in someone else's land and without any children? Imagine that Abraham kept in touch with a friend in Ur by writing letters through the years he spent travelling. What do you think he would have written to this friend before Isaac was born? What would he have written after his son was born? Write one or both of these letters to his friend. Try to explain why you have left Ur and are living as you are.

Activity 2

The people chosen by God were just ordinary people. They were not perfect. They did many things wrong as they tried to follow God. But they did try! People like Abraham and Noah obeyed God even when what they were asked to do seemed impossible or just plain silly. Abraham continued to trust God for many years, even though it must have seemed that the promises made to him were never going to come true. But at times he still became impatient and tried to work things out in his own way, instead of waiting for God's way.

Read 1.8.a—'Abraham in Egypt' and 'Family problems'.

How did Abraham try to make the promises come true by himself? What went wrong? Do you think that he learned anything from this?

Further

Isaac's name meant 'he laughs'. Both Abraham and Sarah had laughed at different times when God promised them a son, because this did not seem possible to them. Find out the meaning of the names of some of the pupils in your class.

Cross-references

● Life as nomads—8.2.a & b.

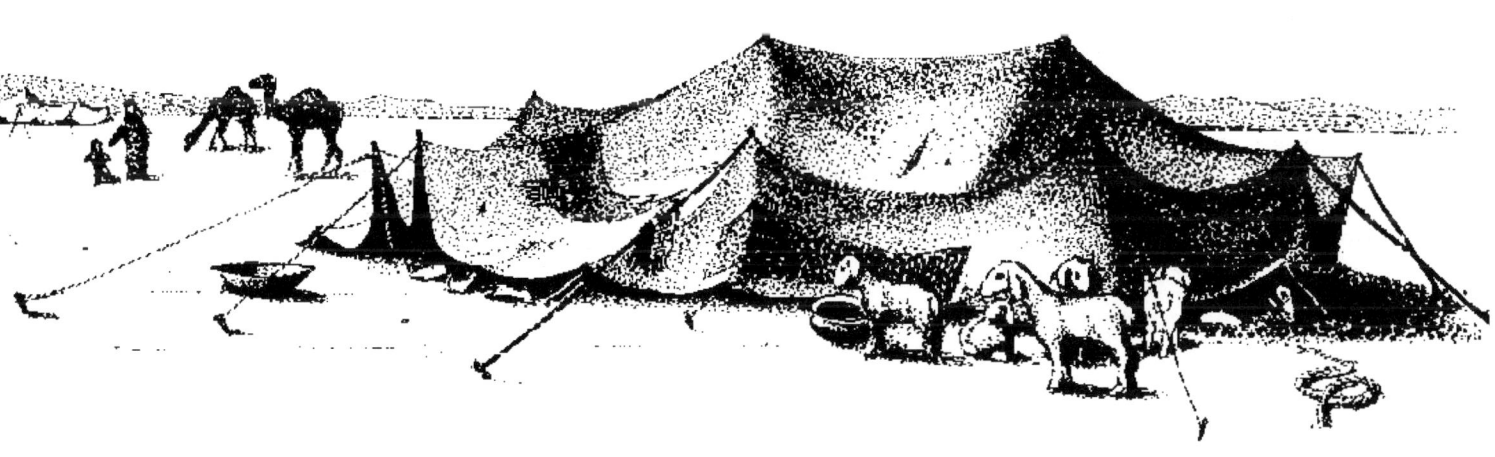

What's in a name?

Family life

Jealousy

Dishonesty

Forgiveness

God's friends are not perfect: Jacob and Esau

Introduction

How many of you watch quiz shows on television, such as… (name a few current shows). Or perhaps some of you have played quiz games at home. A question that often comes up is: 'Name the seven dwarfs in Walt Disney's film *Snow White*.' Does anyone think they can name all seven without help? Ask pupils, with clues if necessary, until you have all seven names written up. (They are: Happy, Dopey, Doc, Grumpy, Sneezy, Sleepy and Bashful.) These names tell us what each of the dwarfs is like: we know what to expect. For instance, what will Happy be like? Or Grumpy? When you meet *real* people for the first time, do their names tell you what they are like? But many of our names do mean something. For instance:
- Philip—someone who likes horses
- Ashley—living near an ash wood
- Hannah—graceful
- Louise—a famous warrior.

If you know anyone called by these names, do you think any of the names were chosen because of their meanings? Some parents will choose their baby's name because of its meaning, but many will choose the name because it is a family name, or just because they like it. Even if they know the meaning, they will not be expecting the baby to grow up exactly like its name.

(Some of them may have found out about some names in the class already; if so, let them share this information with the rest of the class.) But in the Bible, many people's names do tell us what the person is like—just as the dwarfs' names do. Some of the names in the Bible tell us what the person is like—their character. Sometimes the names tell us what the person looked like—their appearance.

Biblical or core material

A man called Isaac (relate to Abraham if they have already learned about him) had two children who were given names with meaning.

Read 1.9.a.

One of them lived up to his name—and caused a lot of trouble for his family as a result!

Read 1.9.b.

Discuss the story—how did Jacob live up to his name? When Laban tricked him, he began to see that it was not pleasant to be tricked! Later, his name was changed: why?

Read 1.10.a & b.

Esau kept his name—he stayed 'red' and 'hairy'!
In Esau's time, the eldest son was very important. He would inherit a greater share of his father's belongings than any younger sons. He would also be given God's blessing—his father would ask God to bless and help him all his life. In Esau's case, his position was even more important, for Isaac's eldest son would have God's promises of a new land passed down to him—the promises that had been given to Abraham and then passed on to Isaac. So Esau lost a great deal when Jacob tricked their father.

Activity 1

 Read again the passage about Jacob's homecoming (1.10.a—Jacob and Esau).

How did Esau behave? How might he have treated Jacob? It isn't always easy to forgive others when they treat us unfairly. Look up 'forgiveness' in a dictionary, and write it down in your own words.

 Read page 77

to find out what Jesus had to say about forgiveness, and write this underneath. Do you think that Esau forgave Jacob?

Activity 2

A famous film director has decided to make a film of Jacob's life. You are in charge of casting: this means that you have to decide who will play the main characters. You need to produce notes for the people who work for you, telling them about the characters and appearances of the following people, so that they can find actors and actresses to audition in front of you:

- Jacob
- Esau
- Isaac
- Rebekah
- Laban
- Leah
- Rachel.

Write a paragraph for each person. (Sometimes you will have to imagine what they looked like!)

If you have time, you might like to suggest some actresses and actors whom you feel could play these parts.

Further

Imagine that there is a law in this country which says that we all have to be given a new name when we are ten, a name that tells other people what we are like—such as Helpful or Bossy. What name would you like to be given? Why? When you have written about this, you can think *privately* about whether you think other people would give you that name or not!

Assembly suggestion

Talk about tricks: some are funny—and just for fun, demonstrate or talk about such tricks (spoon with a hole in it, fake ink-stain, etc.)—while other tricks are played in order to hurt other people. Tell the story of the trick Jacob played on his brother and father. The pupils could mime it while you read it. Why did he do this? But God changed Jacob.

 Read 1.10.b—'The Strange Fight'.

Talk about his two names and their meanings.

From riches to rags...

Family life

Favouritism

Jealousy

God's friends are not perfect: Joseph (1)

You will need

● materials to draw a graph or chart.

Introduction

Decide beforehand on a subject for a chart of 'Our favourite...' Possibilities include a pop group, pet or television programme. Any sort of chart could be made. Ask the pupils for their favourite pet, for instance, and work with them to produce a chart. (If there is time, pairs of pupils could, of course, choose a subject and conduct a class survey, and then work out their own way of recording the results.) As you work, discuss this question of favourites. We are all different and like different things: there are bound to be some things that we prefer over others. Is this a good or bad thing? It doesn't matter which pet we like best, as long as we don't expect others to agree with us. But sometimes having favourites is not a good thing. If we think that someone in our family prefers our brother or sister to us, then we feel hurt. When the chart is completed, read this poem. It is called 'Tom's Moan'.

*My mum likes my big sister best.
She doesn't say so, but I know.
She trusts her to dry the pots,
While I have to read my book.
She lets her stay up late,
While I have to go to bed.
She lets her go out with her friends
While I stay in.
It's not fair!*

Do they think that Tom's mum does prefer his sister? Or is it just that the sister is older than Tom? Discuss the difference. Very often, there is a simple explanation like this for things that we think are unfair. But real favouritism is unfair.

Biblical or core material

In the Bible, there is a story where the favouritism was very real—and very unfair. One of the youngest children in a family was treated as if he was the eldest.

 Read 1.11.a—all of the page down to 'One day, Joseph left home...' in 'The Favourite'.

Discuss the story, bringing out the feelings of Jacob, Joseph and his brothers. Joseph did not make Jacob prefer him to the others, but how did he behave when he realized what was happening? What could he have done to improve things? What could Jacob have done? What was the result of this favouritism and jealousy?

Read the rest of 'The Favourite' and 1.11.b.

Activity 1

Perhaps Tom's sister thought that their mother preferred Tom to her!
1. Write a poem based on the first one, beginning: 'My mum likes my little brother best.'
2. What could their mother say to them both to show them that she loved one as much as she loved the other?

Younger pupils could do the first option only, and they could be given a framework based on the first poem, with appropriate omissions to fill in.

Activity 2

Once again, the people God has chosen are making a mess of everything! Is there anyone here who is behaving as God would want them to? What are they all doing wrong? How could each of them have prevented this happening? What would you say to each of these people if they were in the classroom with you now?
- Joseph
- Jacob
- the brothers.

Write down what you would say.

Younger pupils could be asked to match a list of the characters with the following things: jealousy, favouritism, boasting; the meaning of these could be discussed first.

Further

Pupils could carry out some research on life in Egypt at the time: 1.12.a & b (and 1.14; 1.16).

Assembly suggestion

Talk about favouritism in families, keeping it impersonal. The story of Cinderella could be discussed. Tell the story of Joseph, showing how favouritism led to trouble and unhappiness for everyone. Discuss the difference between having 'special' friends, and being deliberately hurtful to others.

'Trust me!'

Trust

Obedience

Trusting God: Joshua

Introduction

Christians believe and trust in God—that is, they have faith in God. But what does this mean? What is faith? If appropriate, collect the children's suggestions. Bring out that it means that Christians believe that God exists and is real, and that they can trust God to keep promises. But faith is more than this. Having faith in someone or something means being willing to trust yourself to it. This is a difficult concept to present. This story, based on real life, will help.

There was once a famous tight-rope walker called Blondin. For many years, he had travelled around the world amazing people with his daring and skill. In 1859, he went to the Niagara Falls in Canada. There, he walked on a rope stretched across the canyon which was over 150 metres deep! In later years, he did it blindfold. Then, he even carried other people across—one at a time—in a wheel-barrow pushed along the rope ahead of him or on his back! One day, he asked someone to get in the barrow, but the man refused. 'You know I can do it,' Blondin said. 'You have seen me do it many times.' The man agreed: he knew quite well that Blondin could do this. He believed that the person in the barrow was safe. But he still couldn't trust his own life to Blondin's skill.

Having faith in God is like this. A Christian does not just believe that God is real, powerful and loving. A Christian also bases their whole life on this belief.

Biblical or core material

The Israelites were at last entering the land which God had promised to them many centuries before. But the land was already inhabited. (See 'Further', below.) Most of these people, naturally, did not want to lose their land, so the Israelites had to fight. Two people who helped them were very different from each other!

Read 2.2.a & b and 2.4.a about Rahab and Joshua.

Discuss the differences between them with the pupils. Point out that some of the differences, such as the fact that one was a man and one a woman, would have made an even greater difference then than it would now. But both had faith in God—both risked their life to follow God.

Read 2.4.b and 2.5.a & b.

Joshua was the leader of the Israelites, chosen by them and by God. Rahab was little better than a slave in a city that the Israelites had to destroy. But God used both of these people to carry out what God wanted to happen. Both of them listened to and obeyed God. Joshua continued to be the Israelites' leader for many years, and God helped him to win many battles. Look up Hebrews 11:31; James 2:25; Matthew 1:5 (these will need explanation) to see what else we know about Rahab.

This is not the only battle in the Bible which was won when people obeyed strange orders from God. Look at 2.8.b.

Activity 1

Jericho was a very powerful city.

Read 2.5.a.

Think how its people must have felt as this group of travellers arrived at their walls, and began their strange behaviour each day. *Older pupils*: imagine you are one of the people in Jericho, watching from the wall on the seventh day as the Israelites march towards you. What are you expecting to happen? What do you think about this enemy? How do you feel as they begin to behave differently from all the other days? And what happens next?

Either:

1. Write a paragraph describing your feelings during the events of the day.

Or:

2. Pretend you are one of the people in Jericho, as above. Write a poem, describing what you can see and hear, and how you feel. For instance, you could begin:
   I lean on the solid walls, rough stone and strong.
   Around the city, the Israelites are marching once more.

Younger pupils: what can you see from *your* bedroom window? What if your bedroom was in the walls of Jericho? What would you see as the Israelites marched round your city on that last day? Draw a frame like a window-frame on a piece of paper and draw inside it what you could see. The picture on 2.5.b will help you. Which window in that picture is yours?

Activity 2

You have looked at the differences between Joshua and Rahab. Write personal profiles of the two of them, so that people reading them would know about these differences but would also know about the beliefs they shared.

Younger pupils can think about what would have happened when Joshua and Rahab met. What would they say to each other? Draw pictures of the two of them, and write what you think they would say in speech bubbles.

Further

Find out all you can about the land of Canaan and its people. How was their life different from that of the Israelites?

Assembly suggestion

Pupils could learn the spiritual song: 'Joshua fit the battle of Jericho'. They could tell the other pupils the story of Jericho, or you could explain the history of the spiritual, relating the slaves' battle for freedom to the battle of Jericho.

NOTE: a simple version of the spiritual can be found in *Spirituals of the Deep South*, arranged by Ronald Corp, published by Faber Music, ISBN 0-571-51371-9.

Cross-references

- Jericho—9.9
- Settling—8.3.

Impossible jobs!

Fear
_____

Obedience
_____

Trust
_____

God's patience
_____

Trusting God is not always easy: the Judges

Introduction

In 1996, people in several countries listened to news reports eagerly to find out what was happening to an around-the-world yachtsman whose yacht had capsized in rough weather near New Zealand. For several days, rescue boats and aircraft could not get near him, and no one could be sure whether he was alive. In fact, many, as they watched the film of his yacht swaying in the rough sea, completely upside down, were sure that he must be dead. But, after five days in an air pocket in the hull of the yacht, Tony Bullimore swam out to the rescue boat. During those days, he could have given up many times. Everything seemed hopeless. But he did not give in. He fought to stay alive, even though his situation seemed impossible. He believed that rescue would come, and that he could stay alive until then.

Biblical or core material

Often in the Bible, God's friends faced situations from which it seemed they could not escape. Sometimes God gave them a job which seemed impossible, but they trusted and obeyed God, even when they were in great danger. However, they did not all find it easy to trust God in these situations. In fact, some of them took a lot of persuading before they would do it!

Some of these people lived in the time when the Israelites were ruled by people called Judges. In fact, one of them was already a Judge, and another went on to become a Judge.

Read 2.7.a about the Judges, and discuss their jobs—as well as acting as 'Law Advisers', they also acted as God's rescuers for the Israelites.

Alternatives: Deborah

Biblical or core material

Deborah was a judge. She was used to listening to God and obeying what she heard. But God sent her to someone else who was not very keen to trust God—not if it meant danger for himself.

Read 2.7.b.

Discuss with the pupils who trusted God and who didn't. Could they blame Barak? What happened in the battle? Bring out the fact that it was the weather that defeated the enemy. Who did Deborah believe controlled the weather? Read these Bible verses: Hebrews 11:32, 34 and also II Corinthians 12:9 where Paul remembers Jesus saying, 'My power is made perfect in (your) weakness.' Discuss the meaning of these passages: that sometimes God's power is seen at work more clearly when people have no power or strength of their own.

Activity 1

Deborah sang a poem of victory after the battle. This is one of the oldest parts of the Bible.

Read the extract on 2.7.b—Deborah's song.

Age a piece of paper—see page 119. Copy out a verse from the poem on it. These could be part of a display, with an account or picture of the battle between them.

Younger pupils can choose an appropriate font on the computer and print out the verse before aging the paper.

Activity 2

Groups of pupils could each write one of the following faxes:
- Deborah to Barak, asking him to lead the battle
- Barak's reply and request
- Deborah's reply and agreement
- Deborah to the Israelites after the battle.

These can then be put together to tell the story.

Younger pupils can design a moving picture: how could they show a chariot beginning to sink, or the rain pouring down, or the river water rising?

```
                FAX MESSAGE

To      _____
From    _____
Date    _____
Subject _____
Message _____
        _____
        _____
        _____
        _____
        _____
        _____
        _____
        _____
```

Assembly suggestion

Pupils can tell the story of the battle, interspersing the account with the faxes they have written at suitable points. They could end with Deborah's song.

Alternatives: Gideon

Biblical or core material

Gideon was one of the Judges chosen by God to rescue his people. But he did not want to be a rescuer!

Read 2.8.a.

Class Activity 1

Why did Gideon ask God to do as he asked with the fleece? Bring out Gideon's need for proof of God's power and willingness to help Gideon. Gideon was not an obvious choice as leader! What does God's behaviour here show us about God's nature? The pupils can collect lists of words to describe Gideon and God.

Biblical or core material

Gideon called the Israelites together for the battle. He was pleased when 32,000 turned up. But God had something else to say to him; read the Bible verse, and discuss its meaning. God was going to help the Israelites win. But if Gideon went into battle with all these men and won, then they would believe that they had won, not God.

Read 2.8.b.

Activity 2

Collect a story bag for the story of Gideon. You will need objects or pictures to represent the different parts of the story, and to act as reminders of it:
- wheat
- wool
- jar
- candle.

The pupils can take it in turns to draw out objects and tell that part of the story after ordering them correctly.

Activity 2

The soldiers had to trust God too! They received very strange battle instructions from Gideon. Imagine them telling their children about the battle years later. Write their account of the battle, in which they make it clear to their children that it was God, not they, who won the battle. *Younger pupils* can draw a picture of the soldiers with their 'weapons' and write God's name under it as one of the weapons.

Further

Some pupils can read these Bible verses:
- 'What about people like Gideon, Barak… whose weakness was turned to strength and who became powerful in battle and completely defeated the armies of other countries?' (Hebrews 11:32, 34)
- 'For when I am weak, then I am strong.' (II Corinthians 12:10)

Assembly suggestion

Some pupils can use the story bag to take it in turns to tell the story. Talk about God's power being shown by people's weakness.

Caring God's friends

Care for others

Keeping promises

Caring for each other: Ruth

NOTE: this lesson is about caring for others. It is not intended to make pupils feel guilty: it should always be acknowledged that children are seldom in a position to help others, except in a family and friends context. Indeed, it could well be dangerous for them to try to help others in some ways. Instead, the focus should be on what genuine care for others is.

Introduction

Read this story:
It was cold as Liz and Claire hurried down the city street. 'I feel really sorry for people with nowhere to stay in this weather!' Liz said.
'Well, it should be a bit better for some of them here soon, once they've finished work on that old store they're making into a home for them,' Claire answered.
'But I thought they were going to make it into a leisure centre!' Liz said.
'No, it's all decided. Look! They've started work on it already.'
Liz groaned. 'I was looking forward to the leisure centre. There's nothing to do round here!' she said.

Claire looked at her. 'You know that New Year resolution we made—to help people? Perhaps they'll need help once the building work's done—you know, cleaning and decorating. Shall we volunteer?'
'Not likely!' Liz said. 'I've got plenty of other things to do with my time! Come on—I can't wait to try on some boots in the sale—I've seen just what I want!'

Biblical or core material

It is easy to say we care about others, but that is not enough. Liz said she cared about others, but did she really care about them? Real care is shown in action, not just in words. There is a story in the Bible about a woman who made a very famous promise to look after someone else. That woman was Ruth, and here is part of the promise she made to look after Naomi: 'Where you go, I will go, and I will stay wherever you stay. From now on, your people will be my people and your God will be mine also. I will never leave you.' Now listen to her story, and see if she kept this promise.

 Read the story of Ruth—2.11.a & b.

Did Ruth keep her promise? It was not easy for her to leave her own land and her family to live among strangers. She had to work hard to keep herself and Naomi alive. But she still cared for Naomi. Someone else then cares for Ruth herself: who was it? Talk about Boaz, who did more than he need have done to look after Ruth.

Activity 1

God's law did not just say, 'Look after other people.' It showed the people *how* to care for others. Read these laws to the pupils, discussing what they told the people to do.
● 'If there is a poor person among you, do not be hardhearted… Instead, be generous.' (Deuteronomy 15:7–8)
● 'Make sure that you pay what you owe to people straight away, because they may be depending on it.' (Deuteronomy 24:14–15)

- 'Treat people fairly who are strangers or who have no friends.' (Deuteronomy 24:17)
- 'Always leave some grain or grapes or olives in your fields for the poor people to gather, who have no one else to help them.' (Deuteronomy 24:19–21)

Pupils can also use the laws quoted on page 19. Discuss with the pupils what these laws could mean today. Not many of them will have their own fields to harvest: even if they have, would it be practical to leave food in them for others to gather? *Younger pupils* can make up, with your help, two laws which reflect the meaning of these. *Older pupils* can do this, and can then consider how people in need are helped today. Should Parliament order us to help them? Would such laws work? How can we make sure people receive the help they need?

Activity 2

Reread the story of Ruth and Naomi. Tell the pupils to imagine that they are watching a video made of the story, but you are going to freeze the action at the point when Naomi asks Ruth to leave her. What would have happened if Ruth had left her at that moment? What would *not* have happened?

Younger pupils can draw or write about what they think would have happened to the two women. *Older pupils* can first look up Matthew 1:5–6. Explain that this list of names is the genealogy—or list of the ancestors—of Jesus. What do these verses show about Ruth? They can add this to their account of what might have happened if Ruth had abandoned Naomi.

Further

The Law said, 'Love (or look after) your neighbour in the same way as you look after yourself.' When Jesus was asked, 'But who is my neighbour?' he told a story that showed that anyone who needs a person's help is their neighbour (page 79). As a class, draw up a list of people who are their neighbours, using this standard. Together, choose one group of people whom the pupils can help in some way. This could be a long-term project. Ensure that the project is realistic. The following are charities to which children could easily make a worthwhile contribution (addresses are in the 'Useful addresses' section at the back of this book):
- Operation Christmas Child (the 'shoebox' appeal)
- Local homes for the homeless often run appeals for canned food, toiletries, etc.
- Oxfam
- Christian Aid
- TEAR FUND
- The Toybox Charity (working with the street children of Guatemala)
- ActionAid (includes child sponsorship schemes)
- CAFOD.

Assembly suggestion

1. Talk about the importance of keeping promises. Tell the story of Ruth's promise, and of how she kept it. Talk about the results of this.

2. If a charity has been selected, use this assembly as an introduction to this, showing others what the class has done, or telling how others can help them in this. Talk about helping other people. We have no laws to make us do this.

Cross-references

- Laws about caring—9.5 and 8.9.a.

A child and a king

Difficult choices

Value of children

God's surprising choice of friends: Samuel and Saul

Introduction

Sometimes, God's choice of friends is surprising! When the people settled in Canaan, a place called Shiloh became a centre of God's worship for them.

 Read 2.12.a—'The temple at Shiloh' and the caption to the picture.

Men worked there as priests, helping the people to follow God's laws and to worship God. But sometimes these people themselves did not live as God wanted them to. So God appointed Samuel to work as a judge and to lead the people. But Samuel was not given this job when he was a grown-up man. He was given the job while he was still a child.

Biblical or core material

Read 2.12.a & b.

In this story, both Samuel and his mother had to do things which they would probably have preferred not to do. When she asked God to give her a child, Hannah had promised that she would 'give him back to God'. She meant that she would send the child to work for God at the Temple. How do you think she felt when the time came for her to take him to the Temple when he was five or six years old? But she kept her promise. When Samuel listened to God, he heard a message that he had to give to Eli—and which he must have hated taking to him. He had to tell Eli that God was very angry at the way Eli's sons treated the people, and that God was angry because Eli had not stopped them behaving in this way. How do you think Samuel felt when he went to give Eli this message? Why did he do it? Sometimes, the right thing to do is also the difficult thing to do!

Activity 1

Imagine you are Hannah or Samuel at these difficult times. Write down your thoughts as you decide what to do. Will you keep your promise/obey God? *Younger pupils* can draw Hannah or Samuel, and write their thoughts in a speech bubble. Can the pupils think of a time when they had to do something which was very difficult, but which they knew was the right thing to do? They could write their own thoughts in the same way as the above, or, if they do not wish to share their feelings, they could make up a situation for a fictional character, and write about that.

Biblical or core material

Samuel became one of the greatest Judges who had worked in Israel. Later, he had another job which he was reluctant to do.

 Read 2.13.a & b.

Go over Samuel's reasons for not wanting to find a king for the people. In the end, he asked God to lead him to the right person, and he anointed Saul as king. Samuel—and the people—probably thought that his work was now nearly over. But they were wrong. Many of his warnings about kings came true, and Samuel tried to show Saul how he was angering God.

 Read 2.14.a & b, and 2.15.a—first paragraph.

Soon, Samuel was again asking God who was to be king—for Saul had failed.

Activity 2

Write 'personal profiles' for Saul and Samuel. Examples of these—for popstars and actors—can be found in many magazines; but do not allow the pupils to have access to the magazines themselves. The pupils can decide which titles to use; opposite is a suggested list.

Younger pupils can work on this as a class.

Further

Saul was 'anointed' as king. Pupils can research into the meaning of this. Page 59, about the gifts given to Jesus as a child, will help. See also 2.16.a and 4.3.a—'Messiah'.

Assembly suggestion

1. Talk about feeling we have to do what is right, even when it is difficult for us. Tell the story of Hannah and Samuel.
2. Present a news report on television about Israel's first king. Saul has just died. Present the news for that day, using the information in the book and in the pupils' profiles to present a report on him. How good a king was he? Did Samuel know best after all?

Cross-references

- Kings—9.6
- Army—9.8.

PERSONAL PROFILE

Name _____
Lives in _____
_____
_____

Job _____
_____
_____

Enjoys _____
_____
_____

Dislikes _____
_____
_____

High point of career _____
_____
_____

Low point of career _____
_____
_____

Ambition _____
_____
_____

Friends _____
_____
_____

Enemies _____
_____
_____

A champion!

God's friends

Standing up for what is right

God's choices

God's friends are helped: David and Goliath

Introduction

There was a television series first shown in 1969–71 called 'The Champions'. Some of the pupils may have seen reruns. If they have, ask them about it: who is it about? What do these people do? Why are they called 'The Champions'? If no one has seen it, tell them about it. (Two men and a woman have been given super-human powers by people living in remote mountains. They are very strong, so they always win fights dramatically, and their senses are highly developed, so that they can read at great distances, and hear through walls, etc.) Why are these people called 'champions'? Champions at anything are the best there are. Talk about champions in sport, etc. But these three people are called champions for another reason, too. The introduction to the programme makes it clear that they are champions for 'law and order'. This means that they fight for, or on behalf of, law and order. They are 'champions' for other people, doing their fighting for them. This was the original meaning of a champion: in the days of pitched battles, the champion was someone chosen from one army to fight the champion of their enemy. These two fought instead of the whole armies, and both sides agreed beforehand to abide by the results of this fight. So each army would naturally choose the best fighter to be their champion. It is like this when a school holds a road safety quiz. All the pupils in a class will take part in a quiz first, to see who knows the most. Then the winner will go on to represent that class in the school quiz. No one would choose the person who had come last in the first quiz: a champion has to be the best person you have for the job.

Class Activity 1

As a class, make and display a list, describing the sort of person they would choose if they were in an army that needed a champion. Tell them that this is in the days before guns were invented. Remember: if your champion loses, you have all been defeated! They might prefer to present this list as an advertisement, once the class has decided which qualities are needed, under the title: 'Wanted—a champion for Class 00'.

Biblical or core material

The Israelites were under attack from a very powerful army—the Philistines. The Philistines had already chosen their champion. He was called Goliath.

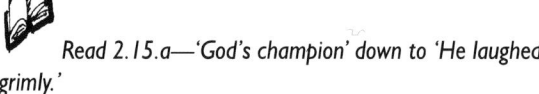 Read 2.15.a—'God's champion' down to 'He laughed grimly.'

Discuss—did Goliath match the description of your ideal champion?
    The Israelites hadn't got a champion—no one would volunteer for the job! Ask the pupils why this was so. But then a young boy came along.

 Read all of 2.15.a & b.

Discuss—did David measure up to your list? But David had something that Goliath did not have, and it was this that made all the difference. Reread the paragraph beginning 'David replied'—2.15.b. What did David have that Saul had lost? David knew that God was with him, and that God would help him. David had learned while he was a shepherd that it didn't matter that he was weak and powerless, because God was powerful and would help him. (Gideon and his army had to learn this: see page 39.) If David was as strong as Goliath, everyone would have believed that his own strength had won the battle. But when weak and young David won, everyone could see that it was God who had helped him. Once they realized this, the Israelites were brave enough to chase the enemy as they ran away, and to defeat them.

In the Bible, God often chose men and women whom other people would not choose. With God's help, these men and women were able to do what God wanted them to do. People were also surprised when God's own son came to live in an ordinary poor family.

NOTE: David became one of Israel's greatest kings when he was older. But he was not perfect! He often did wrong things that hurt his people and angered God. But he listened when God sent his prophet to tell him what he had done wrong, and he tried to live as God wanted him to live. You can read about his later life and his life as King of Israel on 2.16.a & b, and 2.17.a & b.

Activity 2

Younger pupils can draw pictures of the two champions at the beginning of their battle, bringing out how different they were in their appearance and in their equipment. They can write a paraphrase of David's words in a speech bubble over his picture: 'God is with me, and God will help me.'

Older pupils can write 'coat-hanger' poems to bring out this difference. Down the middle of a sheet of paper, write Goliath's name in capitals. Read the description of him, and look at the picture, 2.15.b. Write a series of lines describing him. Each line must contain one of the letters of his name—for instance:

TowerinG over the enemy
He glOats over their fear…

On another sheet of paper, do the same for David, making sure that his belief in God's help is mentioned in the poem in some way.

Activity 3

David had been working as a shepherd.

Read 2.15.a, 2.16.b and 7.10.b about the life of a shepherd.

Write about how he lived, or draw pictures reflecting his life—such as his sling, the sheep. *Older pupils*: God's prophets often spoke about the leaders of the people being like shepherds, because they were to look after them just as a shepherd looked after his sheep. This idea is discussed in 9.10.b. Pupils can produce a series of statements or drawings to parallel their work on the life of a shepherd, to show how David was to look after God's people.

Further

The Philistines were Israel's enemies for many years. Read about them in 2.9.a & b.

Assembly suggestion

Read out the lists or advertisements about a champion, and explain what one was. Read the story of David and Goliath, and use the pictures or the coat-hanger poems in Activity 2 to show the difference between the two champions in the story.

Wise—and foolish!

Wisdom

Proverbs

God's friends are not perfect: Solomon

Introduction

Have any of the pupils decided what they want to do when they leave school? Do any of them want to tell the rest of the class? What did you—the teacher—want to do when you were younger? If it wasn't teaching, when did you switch to teaching? Some people decide very early and never change their minds. Others change their minds quite often. As we grow up, we might learn about other jobs for which we are better suited. Sometimes, people start a job, and then realize that it isn't the right job for them. There are many things to consider when we choose our jobs.

Class Activity 1

Either:
Think of five jobs—as different from each other as possible. Give a group of pupils each job, and ask them to produce a list of what qualities someone would need to do that job well and to be happy in it. Ask each group to share their ideas with the rest of the class.

Or:
With *younger pupils*: name several jobs and ask them what sort of person would do that job well and happily.

Point out that different jobs need different things. People are very different: they all have different talents and interests. People are clever at doing different things. Stress that a) cleverness is not restricted to academic achievements; and b) cleverness means being good at doing something—whatever it is.

Class Activity 2

What if the class belonged to a country which was advertising for a new king? What would they be looking for? What sort of person would they want to rule over them?

Either:
Make a list of their suggestions, discussing and asking for reasons for their answers as you go.

Or:
They can produce 'Wanted—a king' posters, as they did for a champion. Ideas about justice and fairness, honesty and generosity will probably be included.

Biblical or core material

These qualities are all included in something the Bible calls 'wisdom'. Sometimes people think this is the same as cleverness. But it isn't. Someone could be very clever—at maths, or at cooking, for instance—but not be wise at all. Being wise is knowing how to live. Discuss this idea. When someone in the Bible is described as being wise, it means that they know how to live in a way that pleases God. If they are obeying God, the things we have just mentioned will also be there in their dealings with other people. God's friends are expected to treat others fairly, to be honest and to look after others, especially those who cannot look after themselves. (Refer to rules, pages 18 and 41.)

When David's son, Solomon, became King of Israel, he realized that this was too difficult a job for him to do by himself. God asked him what he wanted. Solomon chose 'wisdom'. His wisdom became famous.

Read 2.20.a & b.

His reign was a time of justice and peace, and the country also became very wealthy.

Read 2.18 and 19—except for paragraphs indicated below.

But even Solomon didn't get everything right! He disobeyed God in some things—and caused trouble for himself and his country.

📖 *Read the paragraphs headed 'Solomon and his wives'—2.18.b and 'Who pays?'—2.19.b and 3.1.a.*

Activity 3

📖 *Read again about Solomon's wisdom writing, 2.20.a. In 6.8.a you will also find some information about the book of Proverbs.*

Using the examples given, or some of the examples below, pupils can choose one or more proverbs, and write them on mini-scrolls. These can be illustrated if they wish. *Older pupils* can also write their own proverbs, based on modern life, and can display these as 'Class 00's book of Proverbs. *Younger pupils* could collect some of our traditional proverbs from friends and family to display alongside the Bible's.

'Hatred causes trouble among people,
but love forgives wrongdoing.'
'Someone who does not do what you have asked them to do is as annoying as smoke in your eyes,'
'Speaking without thinking first hurts people as a sword does, but wise people think first and their words heal people's feelings.'
'A good person looks after their animals.'
'Someone who is worried is heavy-hearted, but a kind word from someone cheers them up.'

Selection (adapted) from the book of Proverbs

Further

Some pupils can make a copy of the map of Solomon's trade contacts on 2.18.a and can then find out the modern names of the countries involved. Do any of them still export the same goods?

Assembly suggestion

1. Pupils can present and talk about their lists or posters about kings. How good a king was Solomon?

2. Talk about the biblical meaning of wisdom. Talk about proverbs—modern and their own. Give examples of some of Solomon's proverbs.

Cross-references

- Solomon's judgment about a baby—9.4.a
- Trade routes—9.13.a

Far from home

Standing up for what is right

When things go wrong: in exile and the three friends

You will need

- if possible, advertising posters of holiday destinations—and a holiday brochure.

Show the posters/brochure. What are the people who designed them trying to tell you? Talk about the need to make the place seem as attractive as possible. Pictures and information about activities etc. are used to persuade you to spend your holiday in this place.

Activity 1

Ask the pupils to design a poster encouraging people to spend their holiday in Babylon.

 Read through the information on 3.11.a & b, and discuss the pictures, etc.

What information will be needed on the poster? Which information will they not include?

Biblical or core material

The Jews went to stay in Babylon—but it wasn't by choice!

Read 3.12.a & b and 3.14.a (first column), to find out why they were there.

When we stay in another country, many things are different for us. There are often local customs—ways of doing things—that are confusing to us at first and can even get us into embarrassing situations or even trouble. Have any of the pupils experienced this? When the Jews arrived in Babylon, they found that life was very different for them. The main differences were caused by the Babylonian religion and the different kind of ruler they had.

Read 3.11.a & b and 3.15.a.

Talk about these differences and why they caused such trouble and danger for the three friends in the story on 3.14.b. Read their story.

Think about it

The three friends knew that they might die in the furnace. They knew God was powerful enough to save them. But they also knew that God did not have to save them. When Jesus was dying on the cross, his enemies made fun of him: 'If you are the Son of God,' they said, 'come down from there and save yourself!' Christians believe that Jesus could have done this, and that it was not lack of power that kept him on the cross. They believe that the love he had for his people kept him there, because he knew that this was the only way he could save them.

Activity 2

Design a poster warning the exiles about life in Babylon. This will be like a 'Don't come here!' poster—but they had no choice! *Younger pupils* may need a framework. They could illustrate the poster under the headings, 'They have different gods' and 'Their king is cruel'.

Further

It is believed that the synagogue was first used around this time.

Either:
Research its beginnings and its use:

Read:
- 3.14.b; 9.11.a & b; 4.6.b—'The synagogue'
- 6.4.a—'Reading the Law'
- 6.10.a—'The synagogue Bible'
- 7.9.b—'Capernaum' and caption 'Capernaum'
- 8.10.a—'Different roles'
- 8.12.b—'Learning about God'
- 8.19.a—'Being clean for God'
- 10.16.b—'Synagogue and temple'.

Or:
Pupils might like to find out more about Daniel, who is mentioned on 3.14.a. He is best known for the episode in the lions' den. This is mentioned on 3.16.a—'Daniel and the lions', and the full account is in Daniel 6:1–28.

Assembly suggestion

Use the two posters to show where the Israelites had to go, and explain why they were there. Tell the story of the three friends.

Cross-references

- Background of exile—9.6.b.

The brave queen

Difficult decisions

Defending others

God's friends face difficult choices: Esther

Activity 1

'If you were King or Queen of a country, what would you do?' With no previous discussion except telling them how long they have, give pupils this title and ask them to write—poetry or prose—about what they would do. *Younger pupils* can draw themselves as a monarch, and then draw what they would do around the figure or use thought bubbles around it with simple sentences written by them or by you.

Introduction

Share a few ideas from the exercise. Ask them if they assumed they would have great power, and be able to do as they liked. In some countries, the monarch does still have such power. In this country, the monarch has limited power. The government actually runs the country. In the past, kings and queens did have greater power in Britain. But even then, usually only one person could reign at a time. If a man was King, his wife was called 'Queen' but she didn't usually have the same power as her husband. When Queen Victoria was reigning, her husband was called Prince Albert. He was not a king; he was just her consort—her companion.

Biblical or core material

It was like this in the land in which the Jews were now living. (If the lesson about Babylon has not been covered, explain that the Jews had been defeated and taken into exile in Babylon. Read parts of 3.12 and 3.14, for background information.) The Babylonians had been defeated by the Persians, and a Persian king now ruled over the Jews. A Jewish woman called Esther was King Xerxes' wife and she was called Queen, but she did not really have any power at all. In fact, her husband could have her killed if he was annoyed with her, and no one would try to stop him! So when she was asked to save all of her people, she was putting herself into terrible danger.

Read 3.16.b.

Class Activity 2

Esther's bravery is still celebrated by the Jews each year at the Festival of Purim. Her story is read out, and the children present learn various actions to accompany the reading. It is almost like a pantomime, but a pantomime with a serious message. All pantomimes have a hero, a heroine and a villain. Discuss these characters with the children, identifying these characters in an example such as Cinderella. Ask what happens when the villain appears on stage. Who would be the villain, the hero and heroine of Esther's story? Jewish children write Haman's name in chalk on the soles of their shoes. Every time his name is mentioned, they boo and stamp their feet. The idea is to wipe out his name by the end of the story. When the names of Mordecai and Esther are mentioned, the children cheer. The class could practise this, and perform it in an assembly if you wish.

Activity 3

What was the sign that showed whether Xerxes was either going to order Esther's death, or save her? Discuss what a sceptre is and what it means. Design a sceptre, cut it out and fix it to a sheet of paper using a brass clip (see the illustration). *Younger pupils* can then write to one side of the sceptre what Esther may have said to Xerxes, and, to the other side, what he said to her. *Older pupils* could think about Esther's feelings as she waited to see what Xerxes would do. In moments of tension like this, people often notice things in great detail. What would Esther notice as she knelt in front of her husband? What would the other people be doing as they waited with her? Write a paragraph or a poem giving her thoughts as she waits. You could begin: 'The room became silent…'

Further

1. Perhaps some pupils could contact a local Jewish family or a Rabbi, and ask how Purim is celebrated today—see below.
2. Some pupils might like to research into the Persians—3.16.a.

Assembly suggestion

Pupils could use Activity 2—either as a demonstration, or involving the other pupils. They should start by telling the story, and then explaining the actions and the reasons for them.

Cross-references

● Purim 8.7.b.

Jesus' life

-

-

Preparing for Jesus

Preparing for Jesus' coming

Advent

Baptism

John the Baptist

Introduction

Before there were cars, how did people travel if it was too far to walk? Talk about horses/horse-drawn transport. Travel was, of course, much slower than by motorized vehicles. When the first cars appeared on the road, people complained that their noise and speed upset animals—and people—and the owners had to employ someone to walk in front of the cars waving flags to warn people! Nowadays, when the monarch is visiting somewhere, heralds will play fanfares on trumpets to let people know that the ruler is coming. This is because the monarch is important, and people need to know s/he is arriving to make sure that everything is ready for the visit.

Biblical or core material

The Jews had been waiting for their king to arrive for a very long time. Christians believe that Jesus was that king, the Messiah.

Read parts of 3.20.a & b and 4.3.a.

Christians believe that God sent a herald in front of Jesus, to tell people that he was coming. This herald was also to *warn* people that Jesus was coming, because they were not living in a way that pleased God. This herald was called John. Later, he became known as John the Baptist.

Read 4.3.b about his birth, and 4.7.a about his work.

John's job was to tell people that Jesus was coming, and to tell them that they were not ready to meet him. But he didn't just say, 'You are not ready!' He also told them how they could change their lives so that they were ready. So he told the tax-collectors, 'Only take the amount of money you are supposed to take.' He told the soldiers, 'Don't force people to give you money, and don't tell lies about people.' To the ordinary people, he said, 'You should share what you have with others.' Many of the people who heard him wanted to change their lives so that they could welcome Jesus. They were baptized in the River Jordan as a sign of this. The actual water did not do anything to them. Being baptized was just a sign or a picture that they had said sorry to God for doing wrong things, and that they would now try their best to live as God wanted them to live.

Activity 1

Read again the advice John gave to the soldiers, tax-collectors, and other people. Draw each of these (the pictures in sections 9.1.b, 4.2.a, 9.15, 4.11 and the illustrations opposite will help) and write the advice next to each. *Older pupils* can go on to think of some modern jobs or groups of people, and write suitable advice next to each.

Activity 2

Write a short paragraph explaining why John was called John the Baptist and why people chose to be baptized. *Older pupils* could then imagine they were a person coming to be baptized by John, incorporating this information in their diary entry for the day.

Further

Pupils could follow this up with finding some information about the modern Baptist Church. Perhaps a visit could be arranged to a local Baptist church, or one of their members could visit the class.

Assembly suggestion

Pupils could act out the role of a herald in front of an early car, and then demonstrate the use of a carpet and announcement or fanfare for a monarch. Then they could explain how John the Baptist acted as a herald and as a warning for Jesus' arrival. The meaning of 'Messiah' and Christians' beliefs about Jesus should be incorporated.

Baby in a stable

Gifts and giving

Birth

Jesus' titles

Jesus' birth

NOTE: Christmas is covered in most schools every year. There are several lessons below, from which teachers could choose two, allowing more approaches to a familiar subject.

Birth of a baby

Introduction

(Many children will have had direct experience of the birth of a baby within their family. Or perhaps an adult connected with the school has recently had a baby. It may be helpful to concentrate on one particular baby if there is a possible candidate.)
   Talk about the birth of a baby in this country today. Ask and discuss;
● How did the mother and father know that the woman was pregnant—who told them?
● How did they prepare for the birth?
● Where was the baby born? Was this place chosen by the mother?
● Who cared for her during the birth, and who looked after her and the baby afterwards?
● How did the rest of the family greet the baby?
● If the birth was in hospital, what happened when they returned home?
● Were there people there to help the mother?

Activity 1

The pupils can make a list of these facts, down one side of a sheet of paper. *Younger pupils* can draw the mother and baby after the birth, showing where it happened and who was there to help.

Biblical or core material

Jesus' birth was very different from this. Mary had probably prepared as much as she could for the birth of her baby. There were probably several women in her family who would be ready to help her. But, instead, she had to set out on a journey.

Read 4.4.a & b and 4.5.a & b.

Activity 2

Ask the children to compile a second list on the sheet of paper, giving answers to the same questions, but about Jesus' birth. You could talk them through the answers first if appropriate. *Younger pupils* can draw the scene after Jesus' birth, again making the circumstances of his birth clear.

Think about it

Jesus' birth was not how Mary had expected it to be. Her visitors were not the visitors she had expected. But she knew that God was still taking care of her and her son.

A special baby

Introduction

All babies are special to their parents and their families. Jesus was special to his mother, too. But Christians believe that he was special to them as well. For many years, prophets had been telling the Jews about the future birth of God's special king, the Messiah.

Read one or two of these prophecies—4.3.a bottom and 'Messiah'.

Christians believe that Jesus was that Messiah, and that these prophecies were fulfilled—or came true—when he was born.

Activity 1

Jesus is also special to Christians because of who he is. They believe that he is the Son of God. One prophecy about Jesus gives him several titles (the one beginning, 'A child is born to us!') Pupils can consider what each title means. They can then choose three of them, and make up a symbol for each one. They can draw a picture of Jesus as a baby, or cut out a suitable one from a magazine. They can then make their own frame out of cardboard for this picture, drawing their symbols for his titles on the frame. *Older pupils* might like to read sections 8, 9, and 12 of book 4, and make up some more titles for Jesus. *Younger pupils* can draw or select their own picture of a baby, and then be asked to draw a crown as a symbol of his kingship to decorate their frame.

Think about it

If Jesus was so special, people would have expected him to be born in a rich home with important parents. In fact, he was born in an animal shelter into an ordinary, poor and powerless family. Joseph and Mary even had to become refugees, taking Jesus into another country, in order to save his life when Herod was trying to kill him. It is important to Christians that he came as an ordinary man who suffered all the poverty and danger of others like him. They believe that this means that he understands what life is like for them, with all its problems and worries, because he has been through them all himself. Could they have believed this if he had been born into a rich family which was safe and had no problems?

Gifts

Introduction

How many of you enjoy giving presents at Christmas as well as receiving them? Do you find it easy to think of what to get people? When we choose presents for people, we want to buy something that will please them: something they will like and will enjoy owning or using. Presents need matching with the person. People wouldn't buy a theatre ticket for a Shakespeare play for a one-year-old! But they might buy one for a teenager who enjoys Shakespeare's work.

Activity 1

Match up these presents with the people you think would enjoy them most:
- a football
- a football signed by a favourite team
- an antique doll
- a doll
- dusters and polish
- favourite chocolate
- a baby

- a house-wife or -husband
- a girl in a school football team
- a student in a new flat
- an elderly uncle
- a collector of dolls.

(Some of these are obvious, others need more thought, and could be allocated differently by different pupils.)

Younger pupils could suggest recipients for some of these gifts, or gifts for some of the recipients, to establish the idea of matching gifts to people.

Biblical or core material

When gifts are matched like this to the people who receive them, the gifts themselves tell us something about the people. But sometimes this is not obvious. Jesus received some gifts that did not seem suitable at all for a young child.

Read 4.5.b (not 'Babies beware!').

What were the three gifts they brought?
Older pupils can use the information below to consider what the gifts tell us about Jesus' later life. (The given sections in book 4 will help.)
- Gold: a precious metal then as it is now. Only owned by the very rich, and particularly associated with kings and queens. (4.3.a & b; 4.16.a & b.)
- Frankincense: a resin from certain trees, which had a strong, pleasant scent. It was used in the worship of God in the Temple, and was one ingredient in the oil used to anoint people who were serving God in a special way, such as the priests. The priests' job was to bring God and man closer together.
- Myrrh: a resin from certain shrubs. It was used, with other spices, in the ointment poured on bodies at their burial.

Activity 2

Older pupils can consider what these gifts tell us about Jesus' later life.

Younger pupils: read the above information to them, and then ask them to design a container for one of the gifts which will tell people something about the gift and its use.

Activity 3

Jesus had some other visitors before the wise men arrived.

Read 4.4.b.

The wise men were rich, well-educated and important men. Were the shepherds any of these things?
Older pupils can write a paragraph about why they think God sent such different people to see Jesus. Why did he send both the shepherds and the wise men?
Younger pupils can read the passage about the shepherds. The shepherds were very poor. They could not bring Jesus any expensive gifts. But they did bring their love and their worship. If we cannot spend a lot of money on presents for people, we can still bring them something they will be pleased to get. Draw a picture of something your parents or a friend would be pleased to receive from you. For instance, a parcel of help would be a welcome gift, or a tidy room! What about sharing your new game with your friend? Label the present, and use it as part of your Christmas display.

Christmas people

Introduction

(Some classes may be dismayed at the thought of hearing the Christmas story yet again! This is a way of looking at the story more attentively.)

We hear the Christmas story every year! It is easy to think that we know everything about it. In fact, many people get some of the facts about it wrong.

Activity 1

1. Write short notes listing all you know about the people listed below.

2. Now read or listen to the passages about them, and add new notes, making any necessary corrections. Did you have to alter several facts or just a few? Depending on time, each pupil could work on all the characters; or the pupils could select or be allocated just one to work on, either individually or in groups. They could then share their findings with the whole class. *Younger pupils* could do this orally with the teacher.
- Mary (4.4.a & b)
- Joseph (4.4.a & b)
- shepherds (4.4.b)
- wise men (4.5.a & b)
- Herod (4.5.a & b)
- angels (4.3.b; 4.4.a & b; 4.5.b; book 10.9.a & b).

Activity 2

Pupils can make a Christmas card, using a colour wash as the background, and then cut out black silhouettes of the characters chosen. What colours would be suitable for the background of different parts of the story? Would any parts need this colour scheme to be reversed—with brightly coloured figures against a dark background?

Further

Pupils can think about Mary and Joseph more deeply, writing a list of the sort of people needed to look after the baby Jesus. How did these two people fulfil this task?

Cross-references

- Angels—10.9.a & b
- Dreams—10.12.a & b
- Jesus' names—10.14.a & b
- Shepherds—7.10.b
- Bethlehem—7.16.a & b
- Babies—8.11.a & b.

Assembly suggestion

1. Talk about gifts, matching them to recipients. You could play a matching game with *younger pupils*. Talk about the gifts Jesus received, and their meaning.

2. Or pupils can take on the roles of the key players in the story, and tell their own part of it. They will need to decide together which is the best order in which to do this.

Cross-references

- Inns—8.16.a.

Part of a team!

Responsibility to others

Jesus' baptism

Introduction

Class 4M was in trouble! A break-time game of football had ended with a smashed window in the headteacher's office. 'You know you are not meant to play near the building,' Mr Smith said. 'I'm not pleased with you. You will all stay in this afternoon instead of going on that walk.' Then he saw Adrian at the back of the room. 'Except for you, of course,' he said. 'You had nothing to do with this, as you were at the dentist this morning. You can join Class 4Y.'

Adrian shook his head. 'I'd rather stay in with the others,' he said. 'I'm part of *this* class, not Class 4Y.'

Discuss with the class why Adrian said this. Would he have been wrong to go with the other class? How would the other pupils in his class feel about him now? How would they have felt about him if he had gone with the others?

Biblical or core material

Recap about why people were coming to John to be baptized (page 56). One day, John had a surprise as he worked on the banks of the Jordan.

Read 4.7.—'John prepares the way'.

Then read what John had said about Jesus: 'There is someone coming after me and I am not fit even to untie his sandals.' (Luke 3:16) When Jesus asked him to baptize him, he said, 'I should be baptized by you, not you by me!' (Matthew 3:14)

John was surprised because he believed Jesus was the Son of God, who had done nothing wrong—so he did not need to say sorry or to be baptized as a sign that he would live differently.

Christians today still believe that Jesus did nothing wrong, and did not need to be baptized. Why, then, did he choose to be baptized? Christians believe that it was for several reasons:
● It was a sign that his work was beginning. This was his first 'public appearance'. It was also a sign to John that *his* work was nearly done: the person he had been telling people about was here, ready to work.
● It was a sign that Jesus stood with the people. He made himself one of them. They needed to be baptized, so he did it too, to identify himself as one of them.
● When he saw the dove and heard the voice, it was a sign to Jesus that he was right to do this, and the time was right to start his work, too. God was pleased with him.

Activity 1

Think about a football team. What makes a team successful, apart from skilful players? Bring out the importance of teamwork. A team of brilliant players, all of whom only wanted to score goals for themselves, would not do very well! Write a short paragraph, listing the skills a football player needs. Jesus came to earth to live as a member of the 'human team'. What skills did he need to make sure that he could help others and that they would listen to him? Write a short paragraph, listing these.

Biblical or core material

But Jesus was more than just another 'player'. He was like a 'player-manager'. Make sure the pupils understand this term. Do they think that a manager who is also a player is likely to be more or less understanding when the other players have problems? It is important to Christians that Jesus lived as a human, because it means that he experienced the problems and pressures of life. Christians read the Gospel accounts of Jesus' life, and see him sharing the experiences of people everywhere and of all ages. They see him tired and hungry, tempted to do wrong, ill-treated and unhappy. When they experience these things, they remember that he knows how they feel.

Activity 2

Imagine that you have followed Jesus, watching him teach and help people. An interviewer for the local paper asks you this question: 'If Jesus is so special—the "Son of God"—why does he get tired and hungry and go round with ordinary people?' Write your reply to this question. *Younger pupils* can draw Jesus' baptism, and write one reason why he was baptized underneath it.

Further

Later on in Jesus' life, God reassured him again, saying, 'This is my Son. I love him and I am very pleased with him.'

Read 4.13.a—'The disciples wonder'.

This was also a message to the disciples with Jesus. Who were these? Why do you think they needed to hear and see what happened at the transfiguration?

Assembly suggestion

Act out the story at the beginning of this lesson. Comment on Adrian's action. Explain that Christians believe that this is like a picture of Jesus' behaviour when he chose to be baptized. Talk about him standing with humanity, even though he had done nothing wrong.

The wrong thing to do!

Difficult decisions

Doing the right thing

Jesus' temptation

Class Activity 1

What is temptation? Discuss the meaning of it—wanting to do something that you know is wrong—and ask for other lines for this poem, keeping it impersonal:

Temptation is:
  seeing a ten-pound note on the ground and wanting to keep it.
  wanting to tell others that it wasn't you who broke the jug—when it was.

Older pupils: but sometimes temptation is more complicated than that. T.S. Eliot, a famous poet and playwright, once wrote these lines for one of his characters in a play:

  'The last temptation is the greatest treason:
  To do the right deed for the wrong reason.'

What does this mean? Eliot was saying that it can be wrong to do the right thing if our reasons for doing it are wrong.
  Why do you do the right thing?
● To impress people and make them like you?
● So that other people will then do something for you?
● Because it makes you feel better than other people?

Why should we do the right thing? Which is better—to pick up the ten-pound note and hand it in because we want others to say we are good, or to hand it in because it is the right thing to do, even though no one else will know we have done it?
  With *younger pupils*, this introduction can be simplified. Use the group poem, and then just talk about temptation, and about why we should do the right thing.

Biblical or core material

Jesus was faced with a problem like this when he began his work of telling people about God's love for them. The country he lived in was large, and travel around it was difficult and dangerous. He knew that he would have to work very hard to reach the people. And what if they did not listen to him when he talked to them? Shouldn't he make sure they would listen? After his baptism, he went into the desert to be alone as he thought about his work and decided how to teach.

Read 4.7.a—'Temptations'.

What was the 'right thing' that Jesus wanted to do? (To make sure that the people would listen to him, so they would find out how much God loved them.) What were the 'wrong reasons' he considered? (Making people listen to him because of the wonderful things he did.) He decided to do the 'right thing' for the 'right reason'—he wanted people to listen to him because they saw God's love in his life and in his teaching.

Activity 2

Pupils can write short sketches to show temptation. *Older pupils* could use these to explore the idea of doing the right deed for the wrong reason.

Further

Jesus did perform miracles: but he did not perform them just to make people follow him. Read page 67.

Assembly suggestion

Use the sketches written above. Talk about temptation being a common experience. Tell how Jesus was tempted: three pupils could read the temptations, and another could give Jesus' answer, with explanations about meaning as necessary.

Jesus' team

Friends

Choice of friends

Trust

The disciples

Biblical or core material

Jesus had started his work of telling others about God and about God's love for them. He knew that he would need helpers, who would continue to spread this teaching after he was no longer living on the earth. Many people followed him around as he became more and more well-known, but he knew that he must choose a group of special friends, who would be his disciples.

 Read 4.7.b—'Disciples' (first paragraph only).

These twelve disciples would stay with Jesus throughout his travels, learning all the time from what he said and did.

Class Activity 1

Imagine you have a very important message which you have to take to everyone in the country. You can choose twelve people to help you. What sort of people would you look for? As a class, build up a list of the things you would look for when you interview people for this job, remembering that the people you choose are going to have to work together at times, as well as on their own. With *younger pupils*, read out suggestions for them, and ask whether they think each would help—e.g. rich people; important and powerful people; people who would work well together; well-educated people.

Jesus' choice of people was surprising in many ways.

 Read the second paragraph, 4.7.b—'Disciples'.

Most of them were poorly educated: they were poor and powerless: some of them were already enemies of each other.

Activity 2

On sheets of paper suitable for a wall display, build up a picture gallery of the disciples. We do not know what they looked like, but pupils can use their imagination, and the pictures in the series of books will help them. Beneath each picture and name, they can add a word portrait of each, written using the information below. The class can be divided into groups to gather information about individual disciples. There is more information about some than about others, so allocation of names could take account of this.

● SIMON—originally called Simon, but was called PETER (from the Greek word for 'rock') after Jesus named him 'the rock', meaning he was going to 'build' his church of followers on Peter's leadership. Calling and previous job 4.7.b; home 4.8.a.
● ANDREW—calling and previous job 4.7.b; home 4.8.a. He was a follower of John the Baptist. He brought Simon Peter to Jesus.
● JAMES—calling and previous job 4.7.b. He was the son of Zebedee. He and his brother John were nicknamed 'Sons of Thunder' by Jesus because of their quick tempers!
● JOHN—James' brother; calling and previous job 4.7.b.
● MATTHEW—a tax-collector; son of Alphaeus; he was originally called Levi: Mark 2:13–17, and see page 72. Many people thought he was a traitor because he worked for the Romans.
● JUDAS ISCARIOT—'Iscariot' probably means he came from a place called Kerioth. He acted as treasurer for the disciples, looking after their money.
● THOMAS—his name means 'twin'; the Greek word for twin is 'didymus', and he was sometimes called this too. We do not know anything about his twin.
● SIMON THE ZEALOT—the Zealots were a group of

people who were trying to get rid of the Romans. Simon might be called the 'Zealot' because he was a member of the group, but it probably just meant that he shared ideas with them, and would have liked to see them leave his country. He certainly would not agree with Matthew working for them!

● PHILIP—he brought Nathanael (probably Bartholomew) to Jesus, saying Jesus was the man the prophets had spoken about. From Bethsaida.
● BARTHOLOMEW—probably also called Nathanael. From Cana in Galilee.
● THADDAEUS—believed to be another name for Judas (Jude), son of James.
● JAMES, SON OF ALPHAEUS—(not related to Matthew!) also called James the Lesser, to avoid him getting mixed up with the other James. 'Lesser' here means younger or smaller.

NOTE: space should be left for the pupils to add other information about the disciples as they meet it.
Information about other friends of Jesus, including his female followers, is on page 71ff.

Further

There was a group of three men within the disciples who were even closer to Jesus than the others. They were often present at events when the others weren't.

Read 4.13.a—'The disciples wonder' and Mark 5:21–43.

Add this information to their picture gallery.

Assembly suggestion

Pupils can hold up the pictures of the disciples and read out the information about them. If liked, they can take on the roles of the disciples, beginning, 'I am…'

NOTE: later assemblies can update this information for the rest of the school, and introduce other followers as the pupils encounter them.

Cross-references

● Matthew 10.

NOTE: other information about the disciples is brought together here as a checklist to be used later, to see if the pupils have encountered and entered relevant information. Some information—for instance that about the disciples' lives after the time of the Acts of the Apostles—is added here for those teachers and pupils who would like to 'complete' their accounts of these people's lives.

● SIMON PETER—one of Jesus' three closest friends. The leader of the early church—see page 106. Travelled to other countries telling people about Jesus. Probably killed in Rome because of this work.
● ANDREW—little is known about him. He was probably killed because of his work telling others about Jesus.
● JAMES—one of Jesus' three closest friends. Killed because of his work for Jesus.
● JOHN—one of Jesus' three closest friends. When Jesus was dying, he asked John to look after his mother for him. He became a leader of the church. Later, he was sent to a prison camp on the Island of Patmos. He may have written the book of Revelation while he was there (6.14.b; 5.19.a & b.).
● MATTHEW—it is believed that he wrote Matthew's Gospel.
● JUDAS ISCARIOT—John's Gospel says that he took some of the disciples' money for himself. He betrayed Jesus to his enemies for a payment of 30 pieces of silver. This was the price of a male slave!
● THOMAS—see page 94. Believed to have been killed because of his work for Jesus in India.
● SIMON THE ZEALOT—he remained a disciple. We do not know anything else about him.
● PHILIP—little is known of him.
● BARTHOLOMEW—he was with Jesus for the picnic on the beach—see page 94. Little else is known about him.
● THADDEUS—probably travelled telling others about Jesus.
● JAMES, SON OF ALPHAEUS—little is known about him.

It's a miracle!

Jesus' care for people

Jesus' power

Jesus' miracles

Introduction

What is a miracle? Read the following sentences:
- 'It's a miracle!' said Mum. 'Elizabeth's put her clothes away!'
- 'I passed my driving test—what a miracle!' Dave shouted.
- 'By some miracle, the crashed car did not catch fire,' said the police officer.

In the Second World War, people said that it was a miracle that the weather was calm enough for the soldiers to be rescued.

Reread, asking—what does each of these people mean by the word 'miracle'? Bring out the idea that a miracle is something that people would not have expected to happen: something wonderful and amazing, against the usual. When Christians talk about the miracles Jesus performed, they mean the times when he overcame the usual 'rules' of illness, nature or death.

Activity 1

During the time he spent teaching, Jesus performed several miracles. We are going to build up a Fact File on Jesus' miracles. Fold two sheets of A4 paper to make a booklet.

First Page:
Under the heading 'What is a miracle?' write down some definitions of this word. You can use the discussion and a dictionary.

Activity 2

Second Page:
Heading—'Why did Jesus perform miracles?'

Either:
Recap on Jesus' decision not to perform miracles just to gain people's attention and admiration—p. 64, if covered.

Or:
Explain that Jesus had already decided that he was not going to use miracles just to impress people. Write down each sentence, 1–5. Look up the following passages—either individually, in groups, or as a class—and write down the answer each gives you:

1. *Christians believe that Jesus did not use miracles to make himself famous and well-known. How do you know this?* After he had brought a young girl back to life, Jesus told her family that they must not tell anyone about it. When he healed a man with leprosy, he told him to tell only the priest (see page 73).
2. *To Christians, the miracles proved that Jesus was who he said he was, and that he used God's power to perform them. Who do Christians believe he was?* See 4.13.a; 10.11.b—'Jesus and miracles'; 4.9.a.
3. *Christians believe that the miracles showed people what life was like in the Kingdom of God, as one of God's friends. What was it like?* 4.9.a; 4.12.b; 10.20.b—'A new heaven and a new earth'.
4. *Christians believe that the miracles always helped other people.* Make a list of some of the people helped by some of Jesus' miracles: see 4.9; 4.12.
5. *Christians believe that Jesus only performed miracles as part of a relationship. People had to have faith in him—to believe that he could help them. Who had faith in these events?* 4.9; 4.12.

NOTE: pages 3 and 4 of the booklet the pupils are making are about some of the miracles Jesus performed. Often, these miracles are divided into three groups: the nature miracles; the miracles over sickness; and the miracles over death. There are lesson plans for these three categories. Teachers can select one or two groups for their pupils to work on, depending on their age and ability.

Healing miracles

Biblical or core material

Some of Jesus' miracles showed that he had the power to overcome and heal sickness. In those days, many people believed that illness was sometimes a person's own fault. Jesus disagreed with this. It made him angry and sad when he saw people suffering because of their illnesses. Christians believe that Jesus did not just bring healing to people's bodies. They believe that people cannot be really happy until they have become friends with God. Jesus offered them this friendship, as well as healing for their bodies.

As Jesus travelled round, many people came to him, asking him to heal them. But some could not come to him by themselves because of their illness! Here is the story of one man who had this problem.

Read 4.12.a & b—'Getting through to Jesus'.

In your miracle fact files:

Activity 1

Imagine that you were one of the people inside the house when this happened. Write your own account of the event. *Younger pupils* could tell the story as if they were the man. They might like to draw three stages in the event, and put their feelings into thought bubbles at these three points of the story—when they couldn't get into the house; when they were being lowered; and when they were standing up.

Activity 2

For *older pupils*: read through your answers to 'Why did Jesus perform miracles?' How does this miracle fit in with those reasons?

Further

Pupils could do some research on another healing miracle, such as the man with leprosy—see 4.12.a: 'Jesus and suffering' and Matthew 8:1–4.

Cross-references

● Man lowered through the roof—8.1.

Nature miracles

Biblical or core material

In some of the miracles he performed, Jesus showed that he had power over nature and the environment. Have you ever been in a boat or ship at sea in a storm? Were you frightened? Very often, storms that terrify most people do not worry the crew of a ship at all: they have seen far worse storms, and know that they are safe in this one. It takes a really bad storm to worry experienced sailors! Many of Jesus' disciples *were* experienced sailors. They were fishermen, and were used to spending long hours on Lake Galilee in all weathers. They were well-used to the sudden storms that the lake was famous for. One day, they were caught in a storm that really terrified them—but they were not alone in it.

Read 4.9.b.

Activity 1

Ask the pupils to think of a sunny, calm day at the seaside. What colours would they see in the sky and sea, and on the land? What about a windy, stormy day? What colours would they see then? They can use these colours to make background scenes for the boat in this story, the storm on one side of the page, and the peaceful scene on the other. They can use these to retell the story.

Further

A moving boat could be added to their picture. How could they make the same boat appear in both pictures?

Biblical or core material

Perhaps some of the class have been in a storm at sea, and have felt the terror this can cause. Everyone might be involved in another kind of storm at some time, though. People have often described life as being stormy at times. Why have they done this? What sort of events in life make people feel that they are caught up in a storm over which they have no control? It is partly because of this that Christians sometimes call the church a boat: their friendship with God and with other Christians helps them to 'sail through' or to survive the storms of life. The boat of the church keeps them safe.

What could some of these storms be? (Make sure that this is presented impersonally; children who feel they are in a 'storm' at the moment should not feel impelled to share unless they choose to.) Make a list of suggestions, such as hunger, bullying, poverty, loneliness.

Activity 2

These things are like the waves, threatening to overturn the boat. The pupils can write them as waves, in appropriate colours. They can draw a boat struggling through the waves. Its timbers can be the names of the things that help us in times of trouble—such as friends, food, care, kindness. Christians would add Jesus to the boat: he helps them, just as he helped the disciples. If the church is seen as a boat, Jesus' cross is seen as its mast. If they wish, the pupils can add Jesus' name as the mast.

Jesus' power over death

Biblical or core material

We have seen that Christians believe that one of the reasons for the miracles Jesus performed was to show how life would be in God's Kingdom.

Read the quotation from the book of Revelation, 10.20.b—'A new heaven and a new earth'.

The death of someone brings sorrow to many people, especially the members of their family. The death of a child is particularly tragic. Read Mark 5:21–42 about a man who knew that his daughter was dying.

Activity 1

Christians believe that Jesus changes sadness into joy in many ways. This miracle is like a picture of this.

Older pupils can write their own 'Recipe for Sadness' poem in their fact files. This can either be based on the story of Jairus, or can be based on their own ideas. It could begin:

'Take one sick girl.
Add her worried father...'

They can then write a 'Recipe for Joy' poem, again based either on Jairus' story, or on their own ideas.

Younger pupils can imagine they are looking in through the window of the girl's bedroom. First, they look into the room while she is very ill. Then they look in again after Jesus has been to the house. What will they see each time? What differences will there be between the two scenes? They can draw the two scenes side by side in their fact files, and label them 'Joy' and 'Sadness'. (They can use the pictures in the books for details, but this is not necessary.)

Assembly suggestion

1. What is a miracle? (Slang use of the term, Christian understanding of it, the story of one of Jesus' miracles.)
2. Tell the story of the storm in mime, with a reader telling the story. Sing or teach the song 'With Jesus in the boat...' Talk about the Christian idea of Jesus being with them during the 'storms' of life.

Note: the song 'With Jesus in the boat' can be found in *Junior Praise*, comp. P. Horrobin and G. Leavers, Marshall Pickering.

Cross-references

● 10.11.b.

Jesus' checklist

Friends

Individual's value

Accepting and helping others

People Jesus met

Introduction

Read out this imaginary article in a children's magazine.

Are you particular about your friends? Are there some people you would not like to be seen with? It is very important for your image that you are only seen with the right people! Use our simple checklist to make sure that you are only seen with those right people!
Your friend must have the following characteristics:
- black, shoulder length hair
- blue eyes
- a medium-size nose
- He or she must be over 5 foot (1.5 metres) tall.
- He or she must only go on holiday abroad—preferably America.
- They must live in a big house, with at least five bedrooms.
- This house must not be near a fish shop, a main road or a restaurant.
- They must only like the new group *The Herby Muddlers*.
- They must enjoy wearing the new fashion of odd socks.
- Their favourite food must be cheese and raspberry jam sandwiches.

Well, do any of your friends fit this checklist? Would it be fair to use such a list? Why not? Some of the things on that list were silly, and none of them would be of any use at all in judging whether someone would be a good friend for us or not. But many people have a sort of checklist in their heads. They like to know certain things before they decide if someone should be their friend or not.

Biblical or core material

People expected Jesus to have a checklist like this in his head. He was a rabbi—a teacher—and teachers were very highly thought of.

Read 9.11.b—'Teaching in the synagogue'.

People usually went to them and asked if they could become their disciples.

Read 4.7.b—'Disciples'.

Rabbis were not expected to accept just anybody. Jesus was a rabbi, so they thought his followers would include:
- no women
- no children
- no tax-collectors and other people who do wrong things
- no enemies—such as the Samaritans
- and definitely no people with leprosy!

But Jesus showed that he did not have a checklist at all. In fact, he showed that he was willing to be friends with anybody who needed him as their friend. Here are some of the people he was happy to teach, to help, and to spend time with as his friends:

Read first 8.10.b—'Roles in God's family', 4.15 and 4.8.a.

Pupils could work on the following in groups.

Women

Most rabbis thought that women were not clever enough to learn anything from them!

Read 8.10.a and 8.12.

Jesus had several female disciples. Here are some of them:

- Joanna—it is believed that Jesus had healed her. Her husband was an official working for Herod, so Joanna was brave to follow Jesus and help him by providing money and food for him and his disciples.
- Suzanna—we only know that Suzanna followed Jesus as he taught and helped as Joanna did.
- Mary Magdalene—4.18 & 4.19; 7.9
- Mary and Martha—4.16; 7.16
- His mother Mary.

Activity 1

Pupils can add these people to the gallery of Jesus' disciples.

Children

Many rabbis could not be bothered with children, who were too young to listen to them. Jesus showed that he was different. He thought that children were very important, and he understood how their parents felt about them.

Read 10.15.a—'A message of life', 4.15.a—'Children' and, in the Bible, Luke 18:15–17 about a time when he welcomed children.

Activity 2

If you were one of the children or mothers, how would you feel when the disciples sent you away? How would you feel when Jesus called you back? Write your own account of what happened, using these feelings.

Younger pupils can draw a picture of 'their' child with Jesus.

Tax-collectors and other people who had done wrong things

Tax-collectors were not popular with the Jewish people because they worked for the Romans.

Read 4.1.b and 9.15.b.

Luke 19:1–10 tells about Jesus' meeting with one tax-collector. One of the disciples was a tax-collector too: look back at page 65 to find out which one. Read Luke 5:27–32 to find out what happened when Jesus went to his house for a meal.

Activity 3

Write an account either of Jesus' meeting with Zacchaeus or with Matthew. You can pretend to be either a friend or an enemy of Jesus. What difference would this make to how they would write about what happened? Again, *younger pupils* can draw the scene, showing Jesus' welcome of one of the men.

Cross-references

- Money—9.15.a & b.

Enemies

The Jewish people had been enemies of the Samaritans (people of Samaria—look this up in 3.2.a) for many years.

Read 3.17.b—'Other people in the land'

The Jewish people would even take a very long and dangerous route to avoid crossing Samaritan land! Jesus did not take this route; he often walked through Samaria and even taught there. He told a parable about a Samaritan which would have astonished his Jewish listeners because the Samaritan was the hero of the story!

Read 4.10.a & b—'The Kind Stranger'.

Activity 4

If you were a Jew listening to this parable, how would you feel? Draw a series of cartoons to tell the story, and to give your reactions as the story unfolds. Did you expect the Samaritan to be the only one who helped the Jew? *Younger pupils* can tell just the parable in a strip cartoon.

People with leprosy

Leprosy is a disease which still causes much unhappiness today in many countries. Now, we know that it can be treated, and we know that it is not easy to catch it from other people. But in Jesus' day, people thought that it was very easy to catch it, and they knew that none of their doctors could do anything to cure it. So when someone caught leprosy, they were forced to leave their homes and families and to live out in the countryside away from other people. There, they relied on other people's kindness in leaving food for them. It was a miserable and very lonely life. Most people would not go anywhere near a person with leprosy. But Jesus showed that he was different. He felt sorry for them, and healed several when he met them.

📖 *Read 4.12.a—'Jesus and suffering' and 4.12.b—'People Jesus healed'.*

There is an account in the Bible of how Jesus once healed ten people of leprosy at the same time: read Luke 17:11–19.

NOTE: the pupils will need to know that people who had suffered from leprosy were not allowed to return to their homes until a priest had certified that they were free of the disease.

Activity 5

Nine of the ten men did not come back to say 'thank you'. What do you think the other one said when he returned to Jesus? Draw the scene, using speech bubbles to contain his words and Jesus' words. *Older pupils* can think about how each person spoke his words. Write out the words as direct speech under the picture as well, and add adverbs describing how they spoke. Can they also think of alternative words for 'said'?

Assembly suggestion

Choose two or three of these groups of people. Describe Jesus' dealings with them, how they were regarded at the time, and comment upon what each example shows us about Jesus and his feelings for these people.

Jesus the teacher

Jesus
___

God
___

Prayer
___

Parables
___

Kingdom of God
___

Jesus' teaching

Our ideal teacher!

Activity 1

Ask the class—individually or in groups—to draw up a list of words to describe their ideal teacher. Point out that you will be doing the same thing! Then ask for their description of the ideal pupil—again, you are to do the same! Compare their list about a teacher with your own. Discuss any differences. Include the lists about pupils as necessary. Bring out that teaching relies on a partnership: a brilliant teacher still needs pupils, and vice versa. When this partnership exists, then teaching and learning will occur.

Biblical or core material

What was Jesus like as a teacher? Did he establish a working relationship?

Read 4.8.a.

If you tell the pupils that Jesus went about preaching, many will have their own preconceived ideas of what happened when he spoke, and these will probably be very different from what actually happened. People were so keen to hear him speak that they followed him for considerable distances, and even went without meals, rather than miss anything he said!

Activity 2

Pupils can either draw up their own list describing Jesus as a teacher, or they can imagine they are one of the people who listened to Jesus for hours. They are now on the telephone, telling their friend about Jesus, trying to explain why they have just spent so long listening to him that they forgot to meet that friend.

They can work at this in pairs, and then record the conversation—on tape, or on paper.

Sections 4.8.a & b and 11.a & b will help. They will need to consider carefully what questions are needed to bring out the facts they want to get across.

Younger pupils can imagine they are a small animal whose quiet day has been disturbed by Jesus and the crowds. Sections 4.8.a & b will help them.

What did Jesus teach about?

Jesus taught the people about many things. Some subjects are:
- he taught them about himself
- he taught them about God
- he taught them how they could talk to God
- he taught them about living in God's Kingdom.

Teachers can select from the work on these subjects.

Jesus taught about himself

Introduction

Sometimes, it is easy to describe something: 'The dog is big. It has black and white hair. It likes chocolate.'

Sometimes, descriptions like this are not enough. We want to give more information than just what the dog looks like. So one child might say, 'The dog is too big. It makes me feel helpless and my legs feel weak' and another child might say, 'The dog is all mine. He comforts me and makes me feel warm and safe. He always has time for me.'

Biblical or core material

Through the years, different artists have had many different ideas about what Jesus looked like. Apart from knowing what colour his skin and hair are likely to have been, we cannot really know what he looked like. Cameras were not invented then! But even the people who saw him did not know at first what he was really like—as a person—or what he was like as the Son of God. Jesus knew that people wanted and needed to know what he was like, and so he used some word-pictures to help them to understand more about him. We don't live in his country or in his time, so we need some information to understand what these pictures mean. But the people who heard him knew just what he meant as soon as they heard some of them. Other word-pictures would have made *them* think about their meaning, too!

Many of the word-pictures Jesus used about himself began with the words, 'I am'.

Read 4.13.a & b.

Take one word-picture at a time, and discuss each as necessary to ensure the pupils understand. *Younger pupils* could tackle selected ones, such as 'shepherd', 'light' and 'path'. Further information about each can be found in the following sections:
- bread—4.9.a; 4.17.a & b; 8.14; 8.15; 10.16
- life—4.12; 4.14; 4.19
- light—6.19; 8.4.a; 8.16.b; 9.16.b; 10.2.a
- vine—8.6
- shepherd—2.15; 2.16; 3.7; 3.13; 4.4; 6.12.a; 6.17.a; 7.10; 9.10.b
- gate—9.9
- path—4.13.a & b.

Activity 1

Pupils can design hanging shapes, each showing their own symbol for the word-picture used on one side and a picture interpreting its meaning for Christians on the other side. These can be displayed across the classroom, with discs on the wall at each end reading, 'Jesus said, "I am…" ' ('Life' will require discussion: how can this be portrayed?)

Younger pupils could just be given the names of 'shepherd' and 'light' to work on, and they could produce shapes to go with these names.

Activity 2

Pupils can make an 'I am' wheel. They will need two circles of paper, as shown. On the inner, smaller circle, write 'Jesus said, "I am" ', and then write the names around the outside of the outer circle (see diagram). They can then use these to tell each other in pairs what each revealed word-picture means.

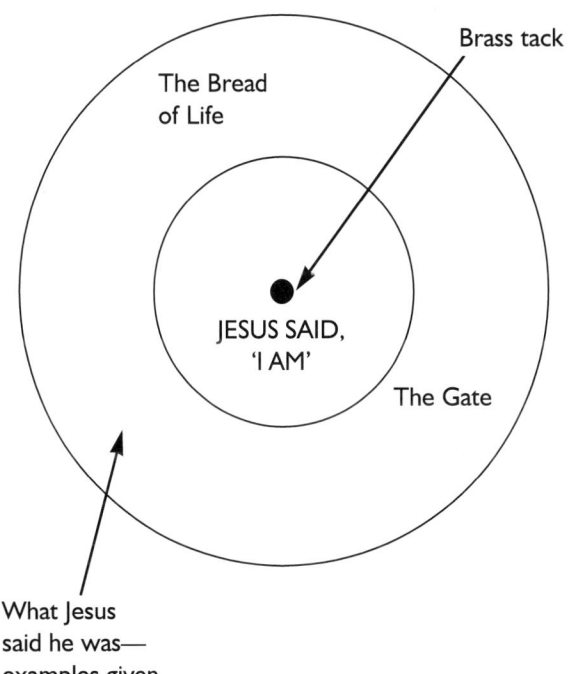

Further

Jesus once said, 'If you have seen me, you have seen my Father.' Christians believe that his Father was God. What picture of God did people receive as they watched and listened to Jesus as he lived among them? (These sections in Book 4 will help: 8, 9, 10, 11, 12, 13, 14.)

Jesus taught about God

In the past it was common to refer to God as masculine. Many Christians acknowledge that this is not accurate: they believe that the good qualities of both men and women are combined in God. Although these books do not refer to God as 'him' (see 10.7.b—'Speaking of God'), many books do, and this issue may be raised by the pupils.

Activity 1

Ask the pupils to draw their idea of God—with no other help given them. (Do not say 'what God looks like', although this is what many will draw.)

Do any of them want to show their pictures to the others, and to tell them their reason for drawing God like that? They were asked to draw their own ideas: can we know if any of them are right or wrong? Jesus knew that many people did not know what God was like really. He knew that many had wrong ideas about God. He wanted his listeners to learn what God was like— what God thought about people, and how God treated them. He wanted them to know that God wanted to be friends with them.

Read 4.11.a—'A loving God' and 'Family love', and 4.11.b—'The very best of parents'.

Activity 2

God is like the very best parent in the world. God will never let friends down. Pupils can use the picture they drew of their idea of God, or, if they wish, they can draw a new one. At the top of the page, they can write, 'The best parent in the world would…' They can then write endings for this around their picture: for instance '… always listen to children.' (You might like to encourage them to avoid personal pronouns in this, so that the work is distanced for those who find it difficult.) If appropriate, they can then write, 'God is like the best parent in the world—but better!' at the bottom. *Younger pupils* could draw pictures to show their ideas about this sort of parent.

NOTE: many children do not have a positive image of parenthood. Some have a damagingly negative experience of this relationship. Care should be taken to convey the message that God is like the 'very best' of parents, not like the one they may have experienced.

Assembly suggestion

1. The 'I am' sayings: pupils could use the pictures or wheels they have made to talk about the meaning of some of these.
2. God: pupils could use the statements or pictures of the best parents to talk about what they have learned about God. They could read out appropriate sections of the books to support this work.

Jesus taught about prayer

Introduction

Jesus said that God was like the very best kind of parent. Children depend on their parents for many things. They ask them for other things, too. Ask for suggestions: list them under two headings—necessary things and things that parents know we like to have. Discuss—is it ever wrong to ask for things? Bring out the difference between the things we need and the things we would like to have. Point out that it is not automatically wrong to ask for things we would like, not need, as long as our receiving them would not mean that the family was short of necessary things, or that we do not expect too much—are we always asking for more? Parents know we need the necessary things; they also enjoy giving us things that we want and like.

Biblical or core material

If human parents give us these things, then, Jesus said, God will give them to us, too. God knows that we need certain things and that we would enjoy having other things, even if we don't need them. And God enjoys giving us things that make us happy. So we can ask God for the things we need and for the things we would like to have.

 Read 4.11.b—'The prayer Jesus taught' and 'A practical prayer'.

Discuss what answers people might receive to their prayers. Sometimes the answer is 'no'. Our parents will not give us anything that they believe will hurt us in any way. They wouldn't give an electrical toy to a baby, or a powerful motorbike to a ten-year-old. God, too, knows that it will not help us to have certain things, but Christians believe that God is all-knowing—that is, God knows everything. So they believe that God knows far more than ordinary parents do. God might know that even what seems like a safe thing will be dangerous to us. So even if we do ask, God won't give it to us. Sometimes the answer is 'wait'. Christians believe that God does not answer all prayers immediately.

Activity 1

Pupils can look in groups at the meaning of some parts of the Lord's Prayer.

Read 4.11.b—'A practical prayer'—and 10.13.b.

Phrases they could consider in groups could include 'Give us this day...'; 'Do not bring us to a time of testing...'; 'Forgive us for what we have done wrong as we forgive other people who have hurt us...'; the praise phrases at the beginning of the prayer. Where relevant, they can look at Jesus' other teaching on forgiveness (Matthew 6:14–15). They can consider why, when they are tempted to do wrong, Christians believe it helps them to remember that Jesus too was tempted to do wrong (page 64). Each group can produce a sheet about their section of the prayer, with a drawing or writing to explain its meaning. These can be displayed together under a copy of the whole prayer written on a 'scroll' on 'aged' paper—see page 119.

Activity 2

Pupils can look at prayer in general.

 Read 10.13.a & b.

Pupils can write about prayer in the Bible. Some could look particularly at the types of prayer as they are represented in the Psalms: 10.13.b—'Prayers from the Psalms'.

Assembly suggestion

Pupils could read out the Lord's Prayer a phrase at a time, and then read what they have found out about the meaning of some of the phrases.

Jesus taught about living in God's Kingdom
[For information about parables, see page 79]

Introduction

Sometimes, somebody wants something so badly that they will go without other things to get it. A child might go without sweets and magazines for months in order to save up for a particular computer game. A family might sell their house and their car to buy a motor caravan in which they can live and travel around the world.

Biblical or core material

Jesus told two parables about people like this.

A man was working in a field when he found a great treasure buried there. He rushed home and sold all that he had so that he could buy the field.

There was once a man who spent his time looking for, buying and selling pearls. One day, he found a pearl that was so beautiful and valuable that he sold everything he had so that he could buy it for himself.

Jesus said that living in God's Kingdom, as one of God's friends, was like the treasure and the pearl. It was so precious and important to people that they did not mind if they left everything else as long as they could live in the Kingdom.

But what is the Kingdom of God?

 Read 4.10.a; 4.11.b—'The prayer Jesus taught'; 4.9.a—'Jesus and the environment'; 4.18.a—'Trial'; 10.15.a—'A message of life'.

Discuss the meaning of these passages with the pupils. Who is the ruler of this Kingdom? Who are its subjects? Every kingdom must have rules for its people to live by. What are the rules of the Kingdom of God?

Read the Beatitudes—4.8.b.

The Beatitudes refer to the sort of people whom Jesus said were already members of the Kingdom of heaven.

Activity 1

Younger pupils can design a treasure maze: at the centre lies the treasure, the Kingdom of God. The maze can have several dead ends. Discuss with the pupils what these could be: for instance, greed, lying, pride.

Older pupils can write modern versions of the two parables about the Kingdom of God.

Activity 2

Jesus was speaking to a group of people who had been defeated by the Romans. Most of them were very poor. How would Jesus' teaching in 4.8.b have helped these people? Write a letter to a Jew who lived in another part of the country, telling them what Jesus said about their lives and God.

Assembly suggestion

Talk about treasure and what it means to different people. Talk about the sort of treasure that people would give up other things to obtain. Pupils can then tell the parables about the Kingdom of God, explaining what the Kingdom is.

Jesus' stories

Caring for each other

Neighbours

The Parables

Introduction

During his teaching, Jesus often told stories to help his listeners to understand what he was saying. These were a special kind of story, called parables.

Read 4.10.a—'Parables'.

Biblical or core material

One of the best-known ones is 'The Good Samaritan'. A Samaritan was a person who came from the country of Samaria. The Samaritans had been enemies of the Jews for many years.

Read 4.10.a & b—'The kind stranger'.

Jesus had been talking about the law from the Old Testament that said, 'Love the Lord your God… and love your neighbour as yourself.' A lawyer asked him to tell them who their neighbours were. Most people today would say that their 'neighbours' were the people next door. Perhaps the lawyer would have said that his neighbours were the people he knew and liked who lived in his own country. Who did Jesus say were his neighbours? Bring out the idea of a neighbour being anyone who needs help, or who gives it to someone in need.

Activity 1

People often say that they have 'bad' neighbours or 'good' neighbours. Who would Jesus call a 'good' neighbour? How would a 'good' neighbour behave? Discuss these questions. *Younger pupils* can draw a 'good' neighbour in action. *Older pupils* can write a short parable, like Jesus', to show a 'good' neighbour in action. Remind them of Jesus' definition of neighbours.

Activity 2

Jesus told many other parables. Three of them were about a person, a thing and an animal which were 'lost'. They are in Luke 15. The parable about a lost sheep is Luke 15:3–7. The parable about a lost coin is Luke 15:8–10, and the one about a 'lost' son is Luke 15:11–32. Read these to the pupils, and discuss their meaning.

In the 'lost' son parable, the father is like a picture of God welcoming someone to be his friend, even though that person has done wrong things in the past. You may like to omit the part of the older son with some pupils. Pupils can choose one of these parables, and can retell it in a cartoon form. *Younger pupils* can do this in a simple strip cartoon, with a one- or two-line text under each picture. *Older pupils* can also do this, but then add a fuller account of the story underneath each picture, as well as the shorter one. (This is in the style of the 'Rupert' cartoons—but the shorter text does not have to rhyme!) This is providing a text suitable for younger and older readers at the same time.

Further

Read the sketch by Jon Webster on p. 81. This is a modern retelling of the parable of the lost sheep. Pupils could either prepare this for performance in assembly, or they could retell one of the 'lost' parables (see above) in this style, working either individually or in groups.

Assembly suggestion

1. Present Jon Webster's sketch or their own version. Relate to the original, with comment on its meaning.
2. Talk about neighbours—good and bad. Discuss Jesus' instruction to 'Love your neighbour' and what he meant by our 'neighbour' as illustrated in the parable of the good Samaritan.

Cross-references

- sheep—8.17.a.

The parable of the good grandad
By Jon Webster

NARRATOR	There was once a grandad who had lots of grandchildren.
ALL (wave)	Hello!
NARRATOR	He loved his grandchildren. He wanted to share a big adventure with them. So he put on his thinking-cap.
ALL (make thinking gesture, e.g. scratch heads)	
NARRATOR	He came up with a brilliant idea!
ALL (click fingers)	
NARRATOR	He would take them all camping!
ALL	Hurray!
NARRATOR	So they piled up his old car with tents and sleeping bags, and jumped in!
ALL (Slam!)	
NARRATOR	Mum and Dad waved 'Goodbye!'
ALL	Goodbye!
NARRATOR	And they set off for the hills.
ALL (sing)	Here we go, here we go, here we go!
NARRATOR	When they got there, they pulled out the tents…
ALL	Heave-ho!
NARRATOR	…and knocked in the tent-pegs.
ALL (mime)	Bang! Bang! Bang!
NARRATOR	It was great up in the hills. The air was so fresh.
ALL (all do breathing exercises)	
NARRATOR	The children were really excited.
ALL (shout)	Yes!
NARRATOR	They wanted to explore, but Grandad knew that, although the hills were a wonderful place, there were dangers in them.
ALL	Be careful!
NARRATOR	He warned them…
ALL	Keep together!
NARRATOR	Don't wander off, and…
ALL	don't get lost!
NARRATOR	So the children went off to explore.
ALL	Yippee!
NARRATOR	They had a wonderful time climbing and scrambling over the hillside, hiding behind bushes—
ALL	—BOO!—
NARRATOR	and paddling in the stream—
ALL	—SPLASH!
NARRATOR	Grandad kept an eye on them, and soon it was time for supper.
ALL	(all hold tummies) Rumble, rumble, rumble!
NARRATOR	Grandad had made the supper, and it smelled delicious!
ALL	Yum, yum, yum!
NARRATOR	But where was (name)?
ALL (in surprise)	Oh!
NARRATOR	Grandad was worried because he knew that there were dangers in the hills. So he told the others to wait in the tent, and even gave them a whistle to blow if they needed help.
ALL (whistle)	
NARRATOR	Then he set off to look for (name).
ALL (call)	Hello-o-o!
NARRATOR	Grandad was used to walking in the hills, but he wasn't as young as he used to be, and his legs soon began to get tired. But he looked everywhere. First, he looked down by the stream.
ALL	(call name)
NARRATOR	Then, he looked in the bushes.
ALL	(call name)
NARRATOR	Then he looked behind the dry-stone wall.
ALL	(call name)
NARRATOR	But there was no sign of (name).
ALL	(call name)
NARRATOR	By now, Grandad's heart was beating fast.
ALL	B-boom, b-boom, b-boom!
NARRATOR	But he was determined to find (name). So he scrambled up the hillside and began to climb up the rocks.
ALL	(call name)
NARRATOR	There was still no sign of (name). His lungs were bursting, but he clambered up to the top of the hill.
ALL	(call name)
NARRATOR	Then he heard a little voice…
ALL (very quietly)	Help!
NARRATOR	It was (name)! He was lost!
ALL (a little more loudly)	Help!
NARRATOR	Grandad was exhausted now, but he struggled over towards him.
ALL	(more loudly) Help!
NARRATOR	Now he was almost there.
ALL (really loudly)	HELP!
NARRATOR	He picked up (name). Was (name) pleased to see him!
ALL	Grandad!
NARRATOR	(Name) was shaking, he was so scared!
ALL	Grandad!
NARRATOR	Grandad helped (name) down the hill. The other children were sitting in the tent.
ALL	Three cheers for Grandad! Hip, hip, hip—HOORAY!, etc. (sing loudly) 'For he's a jolly good fellow,' etc.
NARRATOR	Then they all celebrated with a big mug of piping hot soup! (Name) had got himself lost, but he'd been rescued by…
ALL	THE GOOD GRANDAD!

Jesus the King

Kingship of Jesus

Entry into Jerusalem

Introduction

Have any of the pupils been present when a member of the royal family was visiting your town? Perhaps they have seen such a royal visit televised. Discuss the preparations a town will make for a visit from the monarch—including flags and the royal standard, banners, red carpet for him or her to walk on. Why do people prepare these things? Very often, crowds will gather at the scene hoping to see the monarch. What will they do when they finally catch sight of her or him?

Biblical or core material

What happened when Jesus visited Jerusalem? He knew that he had many enemies there. He knew that he would be killed very soon. But he knew that this was what he had to do.

Read the story of his entry into the city, 4.16.a & b—'Jerusalem' and 'God's King'—first part only.

Together, list the ways in which Jesus' welcome was like the welcome given today to a member of the royal family. (Explain to the pupils that the palm tree had been a symbol of victory and rejoicing for many years in Israel. So it had become associated with kings returning in triumph to their city. The palm branches are like the red carpet, and also like the royal standard; the shouts are similar too.)

So Jesus was welcomed as a king. But in some ways, he surprised the people of Jerusalem by not being like a king. Talk about the sort of transport they would have expected a king to use. What did Jesus use? Why did he choose this?

Activity 1

In pairs, the pupils can write two reports by spectators at this event. They have both been asked what happened and what they think of this new 'king'. One of them believes that Jesus is someone special: they have heard about his teaching and the miracles he has performed. The other person believes he is a fake, just trying to trick the people into following him. When finished, they can read each other's report. Working together, can you improve them in any way? The reports can be displayed under the title 'A Royal Visit to Jerusalem?'

Younger pupils can draw a picture of a king in all his finery on a horse. Then they can draw Jesus, probably in plain white clothes, on a donkey (see 8.18). These can then be displayed under the same heading, 'A Royal Visit to Jerusalem?'

Activity 2

Pupils can make palm crosses which are used in some churches on Palm Sunday. These are made of real palm leaves if possible, but they can be made of light brown card. Each person at church is given one, and many will save the cross until the next year. Some will then burn the cross, and use the ashes at the beginning of Lent.

This is the time of year when Christians look particularly carefully at their life, and say sorry for anything they have done wrong. Ashes have been a sign of sorrow for many years, and some people rub the ashes of the cross on their forehead as a sign of their sorrow for things they have done wrong.

Younger pupils can write what these crosses remind Christians about—the palm branches used on the day Jesus rode into Jerusalem.

Older pupils can add a paragraph explaining why some Christians keep the cross until the next year.

Assembly suggestion

1. Show the crosses, perhaps demonstrating how they are made. Explain why they are used, telling the story of Palm Sunday.
2. Read a set of the two accounts of the day, explaining the importance and meaning of the day for Christians.

Palm Cross

1. You will need two pieces of paper or thin card, each about 1 cm wide. One piece will need to be about 27 cm long and the other piece about 35 cm long. Using the shorter strip of card, make a mark at the 1 cm, 2 cm, 3 cm, 9 cm and 21 cm points.

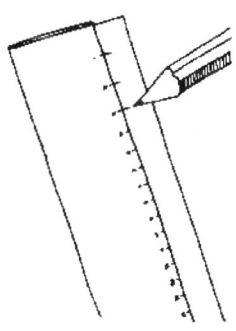

2. Fold the card neatly at each point as shown in the diagram.

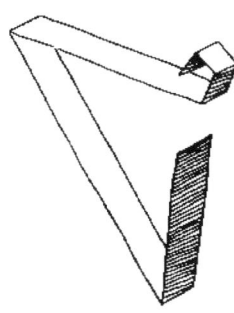

3. Flatten the card to make the cross-beam but make sure there is a gap through the middle of the little folds. Take the second strip of card and tuck one end into this gap. Don't let it come right through the other side.

4. Take the other end of the long strip and loop it over the cross-beam. Push the end through the gap behind the first end and pull tightly.

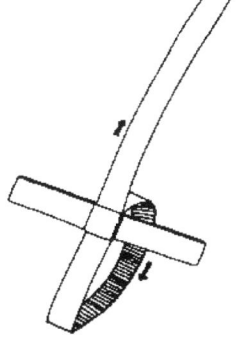

5. Measure about 6 cm along the long strip from the gap and make a fold.

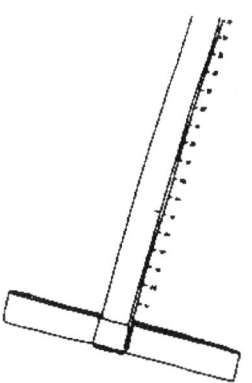

6. Push the long end back through the gap leaving the card up to the fold above the cross-beam. Your cross is now complete.

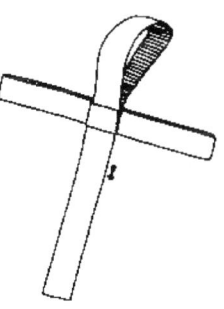

Jesus' anger

Anger

Temper

Defending others

The Temple

Introduction

What is anger? Is it the same as 'losing your temper'? How do the pupils feel when they are angry? Is it always wrong to be angry? Is it always wrong to 'lose your temper'? Ask them to listen to this story. Does it confirm what they have said, or do they want to change what they said?

Darren was in trouble. Mrs Brown had told him that he must stay in at break as he had not done any work. He lost his temper. He picked up his chair and threw it against the wall. He shouted and screamed and refused to leave the room. Of course, his teacher had to tell his father that afternoon when he came to meet him.

That night, his father was reading the paper when he suddenly threw it down on the floor. 'People are throwing wheat away because they have too much to store—and other people are starving!' he shouted. 'It makes me really angry!'

Darren looked at the paper and at his dad. What was the difference?

What *was* the difference? Talk about the sort of anger or temper that is selfish and an over-reaction. Talk about the anger that is on behalf of other people, because of injustice or cruelty. (This anger can, of course, be caused by others' unfair treatment of us, too.) Is *this* anger—at people's suffering—justified?

Biblical or core material

Read 4.16.b—second half of 'God's King'.

Did Jesus lose his temper? What made him angry? You will need to explain several things for them:

- For the Gentiles, non-Jews, the Court of the Gentiles, where these stalls were probably set up, was the only place where they could come to pray within the Temple. (See illustration, frontispiece, *Bible World Factfinder*.)

- The ordinary money of the Roman occupation had the picture of the emperor on it—as our coins have our monarch's head on them. Jews could not take these coins into the Temple because, they believed that the coins broke God's commandment not to make images—or pictures—of anybody. Also, the emperor was almost worshipped as a god by the Romans, and the Jews were told to worship only God.
- Animals were sold for the sacrifices at the Temple.
- Jesus was also angry because he knew that the people who exchanged money and sold the animals used to cheat the people. The people had no choice but to use these traders, so the traders could set their own terms.

Was Jesus right to be angry? Whom was he angry for—himself or others?

Activity 1

Older pupils: an old hymn for children talks about Jesus in these words—'Gentle Jesus, meek and mild'.

Look up the words 'gentle', 'meek' and 'mild'. Was Jesus being like this when he went into the Temple? If he was always 'meek and mild', would he have been a real person? Would it have been right to be like this when he saw people suffering? The Bible says that he was also angry (or 'indignant'—look this up) when he saw someone suffering because of an illness and other people's treatment. Jesus was also angry when he saw people tell off other people for doing things wrong while they were doing worse things themselves. Identify why Jesus was angry in these three cases. Bring out that it was always concern for others, not self-defence. Either as a class or individually, build up two poems called 'Anger is…' and 'But anger is also…' The first one is to list some of the destructive aspects of anger, and could begin:

'Anger is:
hurting people when we want what they have…'

The second one is to describe the sort of anger Jesus displayed in these cases, and could begin:

'But anger is also:
standing up for the child who is hungry…'

Younger pupils can discuss the meaning of 'Gentle Jesus, meek and mild' with the teacher. Was Jesus like this in the Temple? What words would they use to describe him and his feelings then? They can then write a poem—individually or as a class—about Jesus in the Temple,… filling in appropriate words:

'In the Temple:
the sellers were…
the people could not…
It was…
Jesus felt…
He…'

Activity 2

Write an account of this episode in a set number of words: *younger pupils* can use up to twenty and *older pupils* can use up to fifty. Discuss with them the need to show how Jesus felt and why he felt like this.

Assembly suggestion

1. Pupils can read out their accounts of the incident.
2. Pupils can talk about the different kinds of anger. Perhaps they could write short sketches to illustrate the two kinds they have been looking at. Tell the story, explaining why Jesus was angry.

A special meal

Meals

Joy

Sadness

The Last Supper

Introduction

When do we share special meals? Make a list of the pupils' suggestions. Then add their reasons for people wanting to get together like this. Probably all of the meals they have suggested are for joyful occasions. Explain that people choose to meet together over food on sad occasions too. List such occasions. Why do people need to meet like this at these times? (Be aware of any recently bereaved children.)

With *older pupils,* and if appropriate, you can introduce the idea that sometimes a gathering like this is not wholly sad and not wholly happy. When does this happen?

Biblical or core material

Jesus and his special friends, the disciples, met together for a meal that started as a celebration, but became a sad occasion. It is a meal that Christians still remember today. They even act out part of it. And still today, Christians feel both happy and sad when they meet together for this meal.

Read 4.17.a & b—all except 'Prayer—and arrest' and 'Gethsemane'.

What was the celebration part of the Last Supper? Talk about the Passover as a time of celebrating God's rescue of the Israelites from slavery: 1.20; 6.4; 8.8. Discuss how two parts of this meal—the bread and the wine—that had been symbols of joy were given new meaning by Jesus. What were they to become now? Reread the last paragraph of 'Sharing bread and wine'. Can they see how the communion meal now brings both joy and sorrow to Christians as they eat it? They believe that Jesus chose to die in order for them to be able to be God's friends.

Read 10.15—'Condemned to death' and 'New life'—and 10.16—'Christian worship'—which talk about Jesus' death and Christian belief about it.

Activity 1

Cut out the shapes of a glass and a loaf opposite. On one side of each, write Christians' reasons for sadness during the communion meal, and on the other put their reasons for joy. *Older pupils* can then write a short paragraph explaining why the day Jesus died is called *Good* Friday.

Activity 2

The Eucharist is very important to many Christians. Perhaps a church visit could be arranged, during which pupils could note how the church makes this importance seen—in special vessels, tables, and so on. If not, then this could be discussed. Pupils can then choose one or more of the following items to draw and decorate to show how important they are to Christians.
- table or altar
- a cloth for it
- a glass or goblet for the wine
- a plate for the bread
- robes for the minister.

Suitable symbols and colours can be discussed first.

Assembly suggestion

Read the story. Talk about and give the reasons for the mixture of joy and sadness as Christians celebrate this meal today. Show the pupils' designs, explaining why each item is used, and allowing the pupils to explain their decoration if they wish.

Cross-references

- Entertaining—8.16.b.

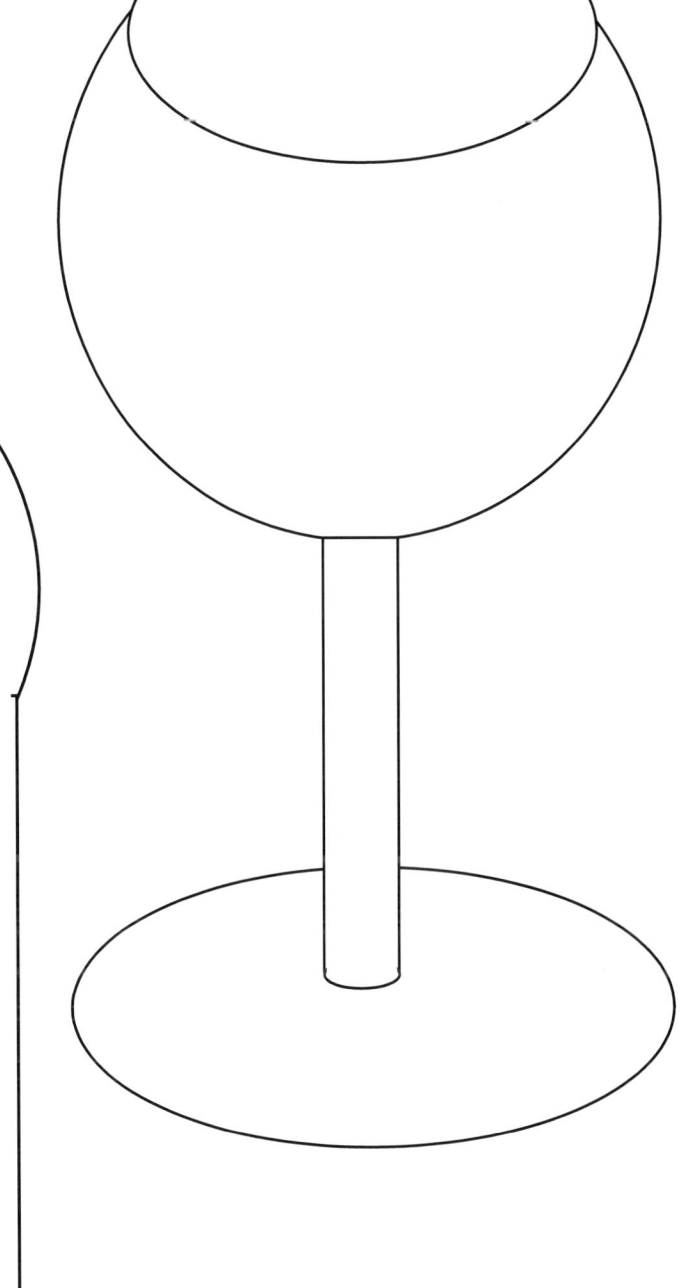

In the garden

Feelings

Love

Fear

Prayer, arrest and Judas

Introduction

Have you ever had to do something you didn't want to do—but which you knew you must do? Somebody going into hospital for an operation probably doesn't want to go! But they know that they have to do it. Sometimes it is something we have to do for others—such as tidying our bedroom! Can the pupils think of any other examples?

Biblical or core material

Refer back to, or introduce, the temptations which Jesus faced. He was tempted to do his work the wrong way—the easy way. But he refused. He chose to do his work the way God wanted him to do it. Now, in Jerusalem, he knew that the time was very near when he had to finish his work the way God wanted. And he knew that this way would be very painful and lonely. After the meal he shared with his disciples, he wanted to spend some time talking to his father, God.

Read 4.17.b—'Prayer—and arrest' and 'Gethsemane'.

The Bible tells us that, after he had prayed, 'Father, if it's possible, save me from death,' Jesus then prayed, 'But I only want to do what you want me to do.' He was saying, 'I do not want to die like this—but the most important thing is that I should be doing what you want me to do, God.' This is why Christians sometimes talk about it being love that held Jesus on the cross, not the nails alone. They mean that he could have saved himself at any time—but they believe he didn't because he knew this was the only way to save his friends.

What about Judas? What did he do? A kiss was the usual greeting between friends. Why do you think Judas chose the Garden of Gethsemane to do this? Judas had been one of the disciples. He had seen and heard Jesus at work for three years—just as the others had. But now he decided to betray Jesus to his enemies. People give several different reasons for him doing this. One reason may be that Judas was disappointed that Jesus was not the sort of king he had been expecting. Perhaps he had hoped Jesus would defeat the Romans. When Jesus talked about love and caring for others, perhaps Judas thought he had failed.

Activity 1

Talk about how we feel when friends let us down. It was even worse for Jesus because he knew what Judas was going to do long before he did it. The rest of the disciples ran away when Jesus was arrested—except Peter, who followed at a distance. They were all too frightened to help. This is a story of love and fear. Everyone felt fear—even Jesus. Jesus' love defeated his fear. But the disciples' fear defeated their love.
Older pupils can write two poems with these headings:
  'Love can…'
  'Fear cannot…'

They can write in general terms about these two qualities or specifically about the Easter story.

Younger pupils can write the two words 'love' and 'fear' in a way that reflects their meaning. They can either use the shape and colour of the letters themselves, or they could use 'hollow' letters and use pictures inside them to show their meaning.

Activity 2

Old olive trees probably grew in the Garden of Gethsemane. They were silent witnesses of the events that night. What would they have seen? What would they have said if they could speak? *Older pupils* can imagine they are one of these trees, and give their own account of the night. *Younger pupils* can draw the scene they would have seen. What colours would be appropriate? Would the Garden seem a friendly, safe place at night or not? How could they show this in their pictures?

Assembly suggestion

Tell the story of the arrest. Talk about love and fear. Read the poems or show the pictures to illustrate this, or ask each class into your room at an arranged time to see the work more closely.

The end?

Overcoming fear

The death of Jesus

Introduction

Do some class work on tones of voice. Ask the pupils to listen to your voice very carefully. Then ask a pupil to come to you, as if you are about to tell them off. Then say the same words, but as if you were about to tell them how pleased with them you are. Point out that it was the tone of voice you used, not the words, that told the pupil whether you were pleased or not. Talk about other feelings we can express in our tone of voice—surprise, fear, love, hatred. Choose a simple sentence, and go round the class, either telling each pupil which feeling to express in saying it, or letting them choose and asking the others to guess. You would need to know the reason behind each sentence to understand why each tone was used.

Biblical or core material

When Jesus was dying on the cross, he said several sentences. Most of these were about other people, showing his love for them. But one of the things he said could be interpreted in two very different ways. Ask the pupils to imagine that they have just got off the plane after a holiday in Disneyland. As they get off, they say, 'It's finished!' What tone would they use? Ask them to show you. What if they have fallen out with their best friend: how would they say, 'It's finished!' about the friendship? But what if they have finally finished a very difficult model, or piece of homework, and they are very pleased with the result? How would they say, 'It's finished!' then? How would they be feeling in each of these situations? Bring out the disappointment and failure of the first two, and the triumph and sense of completion in the third. Jesus said, 'It is finished!' just before he died—but he said it in triumph, not failure.

 Read 'Trial'—4.18.a and 'The King of the Jews'—4.18.b.

What had Jesus finished or completed? He knew that the only way to make it possible for God and people to be friends was for him to die. When he was about to die, he was sure that he had done this. He could have given up at any time, but he had carried on even though his death was lonely and painful. 'It is finished!' was his cry of triumph.

Activity 1

Pupils could look at this and some of the other things Jesus said as he was dying. He asked John to look after Mary (Jesus' mother). He asked God to forgive the people who were killing him. They could draw a simple cross in the middle of a sheet of paper (but not with a figure on it). They could write these three sayings in bubbles leading from the cross. Around the edge of the page, they could say what these sayings tell people about Jesus, and think of some adverbs to describe how Jesus said each one. *Younger pupils* could do this using just the cry of triumph.

Biblical or core material

If the lesson on the Garden of Gethsemane has been studied (page 88), remind the pupils that it was a place of fear as the disciples abandoned Jesus. If not, tell them now how the disciples left Jesus when his enemies came to arrest him, because they were frightened that they, too, would be arrested. There were two other people who had been afraid to tell others that they were followers of Jesus. One was Nicodemus (see third paragraph 4.14.b), who had come to ask Jesus questions secretly in the night, and the other Joseph of Arimathea. Joseph was an important man in Jerusalem. He had spoken out once in defence of Jesus, but had not told people that he was a secret follower of his. Now, these two men came forward and asked if they could bury Jesus' body in Joseph's tomb.

Activity 2

It is right and sensible to be frightened of some things. But sometimes we are frightened to do things that we know we should do, or to speak out about things that we know are wrong. For instance, we should always speak out about bullying—but knowing this does not make it any easier to do it! We are still sometimes frightened to do it. Joseph and Nicodemus decided that they had to speak out. Imagine one of them is talking to the disciples years later, explaining why he kept quiet for so long and then spoke out. Write two short paragraphs, giving his reasons for his behaviour at these two times. *Younger pupils* can do this in the form of a letter, filling in the gaps appropriately:

'Dear disciples,

I did not tell anyone I knew Jesus because I was…
When Jesus died, I told people
I was his friend because …

From…

Further

Pupils could research into burial customs of the time: 4.19; 8.20.

Assembly suggestion

Do some work on the meaning of different tones of voice. Tell the story of Jesus' death. Talk about the meaning of 'It is finished!'

Cross-references

● death and mourning—8.20.a & b.

The great surprise!

Surprises

Feelings

The Resurrection (1)

Introduction

Talk about surprises. Do the pupils like to know what they are having for presents, or do they like surprises? What about surprise parties: have they ever had to keep a party a secret? Was it easy? Are people always pleased with surprises? It can be exciting to receive mystery presents, but what if you don't like them—or they are all the same? Talk about bad surprises—shocks.

Biblical or core material

After Jesus' death, one of his female disciples, Mary Magdalene, had a great shock, which made her even more unhappy. But then she had a great surprise as well.

Read 4.19.a—'Early in the morning.'

What was the shock? (The body had gone.) What was the surprise? Why was she surprised? She had watched Jesus die, and she knew that the Romans were very experienced in executing people. If they said someone was dead, then they were dead. Now, here was Jesus—alive. No wonder she was surprised!

Activity 1

The first person to see Jesus alive after his death was Mary Magdalene. This must have surprised many people when they found out.

Read 8.10 about the position of women at the time.

People had been surprised that Jesus even allowed women to join him as he taught. Now he had chosen a woman to see him first. Write her account of the meeting. *Younger pupils* can imagine that they were an animal—such as a lizard or a mouse—watching the meeting, and write their account of it.

Activity 2

Talk about the 'before and after' pictures used in some advertising. Collect some examples of these from magazines. *Younger pupils* can draw 'before and after' faces for Mary Magdalene—before and after she realized that Jesus was alive. They can begin by working in pairs, deciding how she felt at these two times, and then examining each others' faces while they try to show these feelings in their expressions. *Older pupils* can paint or make collage pictures (using coloured pictures from magazines) of the garden as it appeared to Mary before and after her recognition of Jesus. They will need to think about how our feelings affect the way we see the world, and consider the effect different colours have on our feelings.

Activity 3

Design 'surprise cards' for younger pupils. Could they incorporate a moving component?

Design 'surprise cards' for Christians at a local church—or perhaps for someone who comes in from a local church to take assemblies.

These cards can be specifically Easter cards, or just surprising cards.

Assembly suggestion

1. Talk about 'before and after' pictures. Perhaps they could draw some spoof 'before and after' pictures—but these must not relate to anybody's real problems! Show

the Mary Magdalene pictures, and explain what caused the change.
2. Talk about shocks and surprises. Mary Magdalene experienced both. Tell her story.

Failure and forgiveness

Forgiveness

Failure

Doubt

The Resurrection (2)

Introduction

If someone came into your classroom today and said, 'There's an elephant in the playground drawing on the wall,' would you believe them? What if they said, 'There's a child in the playground drawing on the wall'—would you believe that? Or would you have to go outside to check? Would you need to check the elephant story? What is different about the two stories? We do not always have to see something before we can believe in it. We know the wind exists, we know there is a country called Australia, and we know that we all have a heart inside us. Why can we believe in all these things when we haven't seen them? Talk about seeing the evidence of something's existence, even if we cannot see the thing itself.

Biblical or core material

When Jesus rose from the dead, not all of his disciples found it easy to believe it had happened, even though they had evidence in front of them. The Bible says that Peter saw the empty tomb, just as John did, but he did not believe Jesus was alive again at that point. Another disciple, Thomas, was told the wonderful news by his friends—but he didn't believe it.

 Read 4.19.b—'People who saw Jesus'.

It wasn't until he saw Jesus with his own eyes that he was able to believe he was alive. If people remember Thomas at all, it is for his failure to believe Jesus was alive that they remember. He is known as 'Doubting Thomas'. What does this mean? In fact, he had already proved himself to be very brave. When he heard that Jesus was going back to Jerusalem, where his enemies worked, he knew that they would try to kill Jesus. But he said, 'Come on. Let's go with him, even if we die with him.' Is it fair that he is only remembered for his failure? He had already been a good friend of Jesus for three years. It is believed that he travelled to many countries, including Persia and India, and that he was killed in India because he taught about Jesus and would not stop doing this.

Activity 1

Imagine that you are a Christian in India who has been taught by Thomas. What would you write about him in his obituary in the newspaper? (Explain what an obituary is.) *Younger pupils* can try this too, or they can divide their page into two columns. In one, they can write or draw how Thomas failed, and in the other, they can write or draw how he followed Jesus.

Biblical or core material

Someone else who made a mistake and let Jesus down at Easter was Peter.

 Read 4.20.a—first column.

Jesus did not leave Peter to feel miserable for long. He came to him very soon after he had risen from the dead. We do not know what he said to Peter then, but his next meeting with him is retold in

 4.20.a & b—not 'Farewells'.

Peter had denied knowing Jesus three times. Jesus asked Peter if he loved him three times. Discuss why he did

this. If Peter was going to be the leader of the church, as Jesus had said he would be, he needed to know that he was forgiven, and that Jesus still wanted him to be that leader.

Activity 2

This was a very unusual picnic! Make a list of the ingredients of the picnic: remember to include the setting, the events, the people and their feelings, as well as the food. Design a 'menu card' for the picnic. How can your design reflect the importance of the event for Peter?

Activity 3

Some classes might like to study the evidence for Jesus' resurrection—looking at the various appearances he made, and the arguments listed in 4.19.b—'Jesus is alive!' They could prepare their own statements on this evidence if they wish. They might also like to read the following Bible passage: Matthew 28:11–15.

Further

Pupils could look at some of the other resurrection appearances of Jesus, and write accounts of them. These could be either personal accounts in a diary or formal accounts in a newspaper. Brief accounts of these appearances can be found in 4.19.b, and further details can be found in the following Bible passages: Mark 16:9–14: Luke 24:13–43; 1 Corinthians 15:6.

Assembly suggestion

1. Tell the story of Thomas. Talk about the unfairness of being always remembered for his one failing.
2. You could follow this with another assembly about Peter's failure and Jesus' forgiveness of him.

'See you again!'

Kingship of Jesus

The Ascension

Introduction

Talk about saying goodbye to people. Give various situations, and ask what words they would use in each. Is it different saying goodbye to someone whom you will not see for years, and someone you will see later in the day? Do the pupils ever think about what the words they use to say goodbye really mean?

Activity 1

Research the meaning of some words used to say goodbye—including 'goodbye' itself. Pupils can make a list of these definitions. *Older pupils* can add a list of 'goodbye words' in other languages, including French and German.

Biblical or core material

Talk about the meaning of the French words *Au revoir* and the German *Auf Wiedersehen*. Point out that these words are used when people expect to see each other again. If Jesus had used a word to say goodbye to his disciples when he left the earth to return to his father, he would have used a word like these.

Read 4.20.b—'Farewells'.

The angel told the disciples that Jesus would return, and that when he returned, it would be as a king.

Activity 2

As Jesus left the earth, the Bible says that a cloud hid him from the sight of the disciples. Pupils can design and make a 'lift the flap' card for local Christians for Ascension Day or for a display. On it, a lift-up cloud could hide a symbol of kingship—such as a crown.

Biblical or core material

Jesus left the disciples with a job to do: reread 'Farewells', first paragraph. Discuss what this job was. Jesus did not just leave them alone, though. He promised that the Holy Spirit would come to them and that he would help them in their work. But they must wait for the Spirit to come.

Activity 3

What help would the Holy Spirit be to them? Make a list of the ways in which the Spirit would help them, using 'Farewells' and these passages from the Bible: John 14:15–18, 25–27 and John 16:5–16. *Younger pupils* can write about how the Spirit would help the disciples, as a friend who would be with them for ever.

Assembly suggestion

Tell the story of the Ascension. Talk about Jesus' promise of the Holy Spirit, and read some accounts of what the Spirit would do.

The Holy Spirit

The church's birthday

The Holy Spirit

Symbols

Early church

Pentecost

Introduction

Talk about people's birthdays. Why are they times for parties and presents? What about the birthdays of other things—such as buildings, and organizations? Perhaps there has been such an anniversary in your area about which you could talk. Do the buildings and organizations always receive presents? How do people show that they are pleased that this birthday—the anniversary of the building or of the beginning of the organization—has been reached?

Biblical or core material

For Christians, Pentecost is an anniversary of an important date. It is the birthday of the Christian church—the day it was born, or began. On this birthday, the church was given a special gift, the Holy Spirit. Remind the pupils, as necessary, that after Jesus had come back to life, he told the disciples that they were to tell everybody about him. But, he said, they would need help (page 96) and they were to stay in Jerusalem until God sent them that help—the Holy Spirit. Then Jesus had left them and returned to God. So the disciples were waiting in Jerusalem. And one day…

Read 5.2.a & b.

Some things are very hard to describe to other people. How would they describe diving into cool water on a burning summer day? What about settling down in front of the fire with hot toast and your favourite video after a day spent sledging? Sometimes, we describe things by comparing them to something else: 'It was like diving into ice cream'; 'I felt as if I was wrapped up in a woolly blanket.'

At Pentecost, it seemed to the disciples that the Holy Spirit came to them as fire and as wind. These are symbols of the Spirit. Why are they used? (10.17) Talk about the attributes of fire: it is powerful, cleansing. What about the wind? This is unseen but powerful. What do these symbols tell us about the Holy Spirit? Another symbol that is used to represent the Spirit is that of a dove. What does this symbol say about the Spirit?

Read 4.20.b and 5.2.

Find out what the Holy Spirit was going to do for the disciples. Which job belongs with which symbol?

Activity 1

Make a mobile of one of the symbols of the Holy Spirit, or combine all three. What colours will be appropriate for each symbol? Discuss with the pupils where these could be hung in order for the 'wind' or draught to move them and to remind them that the Spirit is likened to the wind. (This could be in a draught from a door or window, or over a radiator to catch the warm air rising.)

Activity 2

Design a Pentecost Day card for the birthday of the church. Perhaps these could be given to a local church, or to a friend of the school who is a Christian. Which symbols do the pupils think they should use? They could draw or mount these on a colour wash background: which colours would be suitable for this?

Further

Pentecost was not always a Christian festival. Use the books to find out what the Feast of Pentecost was originally. What is this called now?

Assembly suggestion

Show the mobiles and cards and explain why these have been made, telling the story of the coming of the Holy Spirit. Explain the symbols used.

Jesus' teaching about the Holy Spirit

Gifts of the Holy Spirit

Spiritual gifts

Introduction

Recap on the coming of the Holy Spirit—page 99 and 5.2.

Biblical or core material

This day is called the birthday of the church, because it was the day when other people joined the disciples. Usually, gifts are given to the person whose birthday it is, and the church was given gifts at Pentecost. Jesus had told the disciples what the Holy Spirit would do for them. He said the Spirit would teach them what to say, help them when they were in danger, remind them of Jesus' own teaching, and stay with them for ever. After Pentecost, the disciples experienced the Spirit doing all of these things. Several of them were also able to do amazing things because of the Spirit's power within them:

 Read 5.2.b.

Peter was able to heal a man who had not been able to walk.

 Read 10.17.b—'God's Spirit in Christians'.

This ends with the list of the special qualities that Christians believe the Spirit produces in them.

 Then read 5.10.b—'Spiritual gifts'.

Discuss all of these 'gifts' that Christians believe the Holy Spirit gives to them.

Activity 1

Talk about gifts. Gifts do not have to be 'useful'. If someone says, 'That is just what I wanted', the gift they are talking about need not be useful; it could just be something they really wanted to have. The gifts the disciples received at Pentecost were just what they wanted and just what they needed! Make a 'present' from the Holy Spirit: cut a square of paper as shown. The paper could be wrapping paper, or it could be plain paper decorated on one side by the pupils. (They could use the symbols of the Holy Spirit to decorate it—see page 99.) Fold as shown.

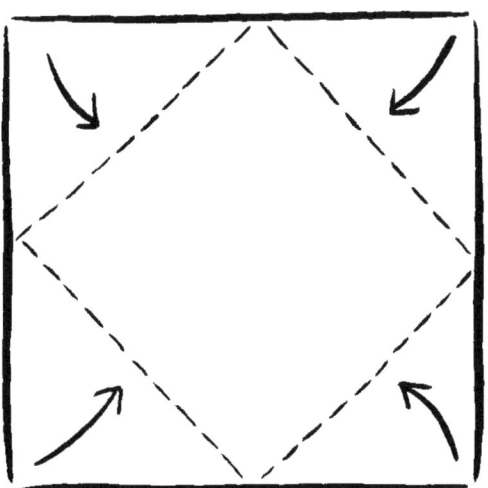

On the central square inside, they should each write one of the gifts the Spirit gave to the disciples—for instance 'The Spirit helped them to talk to people about God.' Lengths of narrow ribbon or thread can be used to tie up the presents, and they can then be displayed on the wall under the heading 'Christians believe the Holy Spirit gives them these gifts'.

Assembly suggestion

Talk about Pentecost being the birthday of the church. Show the Holy Spirit gifts, and talk about each one.

Activity 2

Make a 'wheel' about the fruit of the Holy Spirit, as on pages 25 and 75. The inner disc should say, 'The Spirit gives…' The fruit listed on 10.17.b should be on the outer disc. The idea of this fruit being singular even while it has many facets can be reflected in a drawing of a bunch of grapes to decorate the inner disc. *Older pupils* can discuss and write about the meaning of each quality mentioned. These paragraphs could be displayed around the wheels.

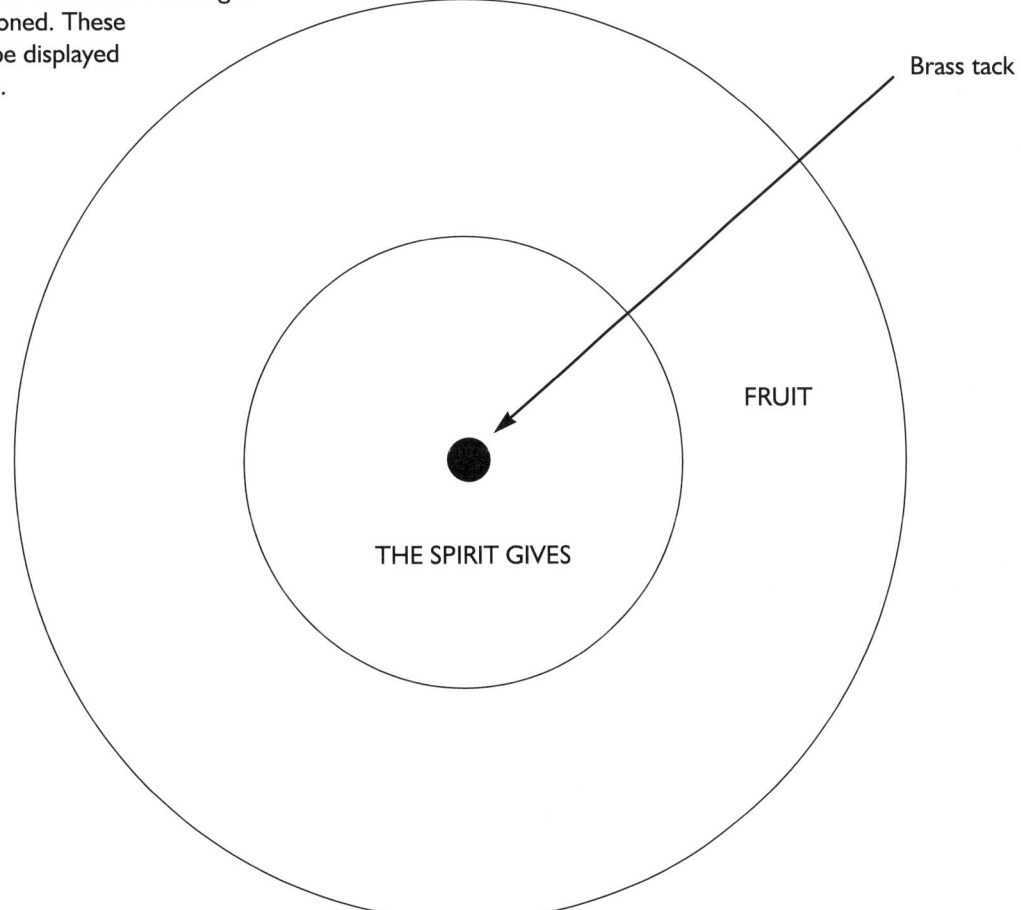

The Helper

The Holy Spirit

Symbols

The Holy Spirit

Biblical or core material

The Holy Spirit came to the disciples at Pentecost. But this was not the first time the Spirit had been active in the Bible, and it was certainly not the last.

Activity 1

Older pupils can look up the following references and write about the actions and work of the Holy Spirit. *Younger pupils* can read through the passages with the teacher, and can illustrate one or more of the events mentioned:
- Creation—10.17.a
- The Prophets—10.17.a
- Zechariah—10.17.b
- Ezekiel—Ezekiel 37:1–14. (This is the story of Ezekiel's vision of the valley of dry bones, in which God used this imagery to show how the Spirit would bring new life to his people. *Older pupils* could use this reference, but they will need some commentary about it.)
- Jesus' baptism—4.7.a; page 62.

Activity 2

Bring together the work done on the symbols used for the Holy Spirit by writing poems about one or more of the above events which describe the work of the Spirit in terms of the symbols.

Read page 98.

Remind the pupils of the use of the symbols wind, fire and dove. Encourage them to consider which symbol(s) best match each event. A poem could begin:
> Creation
> Like a dove the Spirit hovered,
> Wings outstretched over darkness…

and continue:
> But then, like the wind,
> The Spirit's power was released…

Younger pupils can draw each symbol in turn, and then think of words to describe that symbol. They can end each picture by completing: 'The Holy Spirit was like this when…' if they wish.

Assembly suggestion

Pupils can choose one or more episodes of the Spirit's activity to describe, and can use their poems or pictures to talk about the imagery used to help people in their perception of the Spirit.

Early church

Growth—and a death

Early church

Stephen

Martyrs

Growth

The early church and Stephen

You will need

- A week before this lesson, grow some cress or beansprouts with the pupils if possible.
- Or, show seeds and a picture of the plant they will grow into.

Introduction

If it has not been possible to grow anything, show the seeds and the picture, and talk about the rapid growth of plants from tiny seeds. If the pupils have grown anything, show these and talk about the change. When Jesus was talking about the Kingdom of God (see page 77), he said that it would grow just as a mustard plant grows from a very small seed. And that is just what the disciples saw happening in the weeks after Jesus had left them.

Biblical or core material

The church was growing! It began with the disciples—now known as the apostles (5.16.b) and the other people who had followed Jesus as he worked. Then, on the day of Pentecost, 3,000 people became Christians. Now the church was growing all the time.

Read the first paragraph on 5.3.a, the first paragraph on 5.10.a and 'Meeting for worship' and 'Spiritual gifts' on 5.10.b.

The early Christians would also share all they had, so that nobody was hungry or without a place to live.

Activity 1

The first Christians were very busy people! Write four entries for the diary of one of them, giving a picture of how they spent their days. Remember, they had their families to look after, and their normal work to do as well! *Younger pupils* can draw these entries from their diaries. Pupils can use Books 8 and 9 to choose a suitable job if they need to.

Biblical or core material

But not everyone was pleased about the growth of the church.

Read 5.3.a—'Hard questions'.

Opposition increased, and soon one of the deacons was in trouble.

Read 5.3.b—'Seven Deacons'—and then the story of Stephen, on the same page.

Activity 2

Older pupils can continue with their diaries, giving their account of what happened to Stephen. *Younger pupils* can draw what happened to another deacon, Philip.

Read 5.1.b—'Philip and the Ethiopian'.

104

Further

Some pupils could find out what happened to Judas after he betrayed Jesus, and then find out who the disciples appointed in his place: 5.2.a and Acts 1:20–26.

Assembly suggestion

Pupils can show the seeds they have grown, or seeds and pictures of the plants into which they grow. Talk about rapid growth, and tell how the church grew from small beginnings.

Success and failure
Early church

Success
___

Failure
___

Peter's life

Introduction

Who likes 'white-knuckle' rides? Why are they called this? What are the frightening parts of your favourites? Many of these rides are based on the basic idea of a roller-coaster. Ensure all the children understand this basic idea—of rapid movements up and down following each other in quick succession. Sometimes, life seems like a roller-coaster ride. We have a good day when everything goes well, and then the next day is miserable—no one talks to us, and the maths is too hard for us to do!

Biblical or core material

Peter was one of the first disciples Jesus chose. He and the others were given a vital job by Jesus when he left the earth to return to God. They were to tell other people about Jesus and his love for them. If they had failed, who else could have done this? They had been with Jesus throughout his work, and had seen him die. They had met him when he came back to life. Jesus was depending on them. What sort of people do you think he chose? If they have already done the work on the disciples, remind them of this: the disciples were just ordinary people, with little education and little money and power. They were ordinary in other ways too. They were not perfect: they often got things wrong. Peter, especially, often did things wrong. He was very good at acting without thinking. He made promises he could not keep. He let Jesus down. But at the same time, he often saw things—about Jesus—that other people did not understand. He went on to become one of the most important leaders of the early church. But his life was a series of 'ups' and 'downs': it was, in fact, like a roller-coaster!

Go through the following events in Peter's life, briefly describing them and asking the pupils whether each one was a highpoint or a lowpoint of Peter's career:
- calling— 4.7; 4.14.a
- walking on water—Matthew 14:22–29
- sinking—Matthew 14:30–33
- confessing—4.13.a
- one of the three—6.12.a; Luke 8:40–56
- promising—Luke 22.33
- denying—4.20.a
- seeing Jesus—I Corinthians 15:5; page 94
- commission—4.20
- Pentecost—5.2
- speech—5.2
- vision—5.5
- leadership—5.2; 5.3; 5.5; 5.7
- healing—Acts 3:1–10.

Activity 1

Design a roller-coaster of Peter's life! Make two lists—one of the high points in his life, and one of the low points. Now decide which were the best high points—his greatest achievements—and which were the worst low points—his worst failures. These will be the highest and lowest points on the roller-coaster ride. Design the ride. Think about Peter's feelings during the events. Can you use other parts of the ride—such as looping the loop, darkness, water—to reflect his feelings? Draw the ride in any way you like. Probably the easiest way is to draw it as if you are standing at its side, looking at it. You must label the ride so that people know which events match each part of the ride. How will you do this? Think about a name for the ride. Then can you think of a phrase to go with it which tells people that Peter was a great leader, even though he was not perfect? (For instance, 'Peter, the successful failure'.)

Activity 2

Peter must have felt he was on a roller-coaster ride at times; his feelings changed so quickly and so greatly.

Imagine that you are Peter. Choose a success and a failure from the list above. Write your diary entries for each event, describing both what happened, and your feelings about the events. How could you decorate (not illustrate) the two entries to reflect the feelings described in them? *Younger pupils* could illustrate the two events they choose.

Further

Pupils can use the Books to research into the food laws which are referred to in Peter's vision—5.5. They will find information on 5.7. Alternatively, they can use 5.7 to consider how Jews and Gentiles regarded each other at the time.

Assembly suggestion

Pupils can mime a roller-coaster ride, with an account of some of the events of Peter's life: some can pretend to be on the ride, freeze-framing the action at a high or low point while others tell the story of that event.

Cross-references

- Peter's vision—8.1.a & b.

An enemy who became a friend

Early church

Paul

Change

Encouragement

Paul

Introduction

People often talk about a 'turning-point' in their lives. They mean a certain time or event which changed their lives completely. A parent might say that the birth of their first child was a turning-point, or a child might say that discovering they were good at tennis was a turning-point. The Bible has many stories about people who experienced turning-points in their lives, after which their lives were never the same again. Killing Goliath was such an event for David! Mary's life was never the same after the angel told her she was going to have a baby. Very often in the Bible, the turning-point comes when a person meets God for the first time.

Biblical or core material

When Stephen was killed because of his belief in Jesus, there was a man watching called Saul.

  Read 5.4.a—first column, and b—'Saul and his family' and 'Roman citizens'.

Saul was convinced that the Christians were wrong about Jesus. He believed that Jesus had been just an ordinary man, and his followers were tricking people when they said he was someone special. He was determined to show these people how wrong they were, so that they would return to their old way of life. Saul was on his way to the city of Damascus to persecute Christians when he had an experience which marked a turning point in his life.

Read 5.4.a & b.

After this, everyone turned against Saul for a while. The Christians were afraid that he was pretending to be a Christian to trick them into revealing themselves, and the Jews were furious that this man, who had worked so hard to get rid of the Christians, was now joining them! When he travelled to Jerusalem to join the Christians there, they did not want him at first! But then a man called Barnabas spoke up for him, persuading the others that they could trust him. Barnabas later travelled with Saul to tell others about Jesus.

Read 5.4.b—'Did you know?' about Saul's change of name.

Activity 1

Write two acrostic poems about Saul before and after his experience on the way to Damascus. Discuss which events and type of behaviour belong to which period. The differences could be accentuated by using the two forms of his name—Saul for the first poem, and Paul for the second. These poems do not have to rhyme. The first one could begin:
*Seeking out the believers in Jesus,
Angrily…*

Younger pupils could draw two faces of Saul. They could label the first one Saul and complete the sentence underneath: 'I want to…' The other one could be labelled Paul, and again they could complete the sentence 'I want to…' underneath it.

Activity 2

What does 'encouragement' mean? Do we all need it? Are there times when we need it more than at others? Barnabas was well-known at the time for the encouragement he gave to others: he was known as 'the Son of Encouragement' or 'the man who encourages others.' How can we encourage other people? It is very easy to criticize other people, and to do the opposite to encouraging them! Put the name of each pupil on a small piece of paper. Put these in a bowl. Explain that they are going to take one piece of paper each—no swapping or comments allowed! They are to think of one positive thing to say about that person. Stress the 'positive'! They could start, 'I like…' or 'I am impressed by…' These comments can be displayed on a board headed: 'Our Barnabas Board: we encourage each other, just as Barnabas did.'

The pupils might like to draw themselves to accompany the comments, or they could write their name using different decorative scripts on the computer. You might like to invite them to add any further positive comments during the week, and/or to add any yourself.

Further

What happened to Barnabas? Some pupils might like to use the books to find out all they can about Barnabas and his work.

Assembly suggestion

Discuss how you have used the Barnabas Board, explaining its name. Tell the others why encouragement is a good thing in a school. How does it make them feel?

The travelling teacher

Paul

Paul's missionary journeys

NOTE: this is a large topic. A way of dealing with it is suggested which will help the pupils to see the overall pattern of Paul's work without becoming bogged down in the details of the journeys and routes. (If preferred, individual events and people can be studied by themselves.)

Introduction

Why do people go on journeys? Usually, it is in order to reach somewhere—as when we go on holiday. Sometimes, the journey itself is the main thing—as on a touring holiday. Sometimes, people go on journeys because they have special news to tell their family or friends—news that they do not want to write in a letter, or tell on the telephone. It might be good or bad news that they want to tell to others face to face like this. Can they think of any examples? Few people would set off on a long and dangerous journey to tell any news to complete strangers. Can they think of any cases where this might happen? (For instance, to warn people of something like an earthquake, etc.)

Biblical or core material

Nowadays, journeys in most countries are safe. After his experience of meeting Jesus on the way to Damascus, Paul spent several years finding out all that Jesus wanted him to know. Then he began his work for him. He set off on a series of journeys to tell other people his good news—that Jesus was alive and that he cared for them. These people were strangers to him, and he was often in great danger. But he refused to stop telling people about Jesus. Here is what he said about his journeys and his work for Jesus:

'We have been treated cruelly and unfairly. We have been hungry, thirsty, and without rest. I have been shipwrecked, thrown into prison, whipped and stoned. But through it all, I have had the most important things—the love of God and the knowledge that I have been doing what he asked me to do. Knowing God loves me and that I am working for him is far more important than all of these troubles.'

II Corinthians 11:16–33 (adapted)

Let's find out a bit more about these journeys.

You will need

● a large map of the area of Paul's journeys—see the one provided. This will form the basis of the work, and should be displayed with room around it for the pupils' contributions;
● Blu-tak and thread—in different colours
● a pen that will write on the map while it is on the wall
● a modern atlas
● smaller practice maps for some of the groups.

Working on independent projects in groups, the pupils will build up a map of the journeys, with key events highlighted. They could, of course, work individually, or on fewer of the suggested projects as a whole class.

Class Activity 1

Begin by putting on the map the names of the countries and regions involved: Macedonia, Syria, Italy, Galatia, Asia, Mediterranean Sea, Cyprus, Pisidia, Pamphylia, Cilicia, Sicily, Malta, Crete. See maps in sections 5.6, 8 and 13.

1. Events and people: some of these are detailed below. The groups can choose one to research. They write a paragraph about it, telling the others what happened and why. This is then located on the map, using thread and Blu-tak, the thread leading to their paragraph fastened to the display around the map.

Events and people
● Paul and Barnabas set off—6.a.
● An important meeting at Jerusalem—7.a & b.
● Luke joins Paul—8.a, 16.a and see 6.13 b.

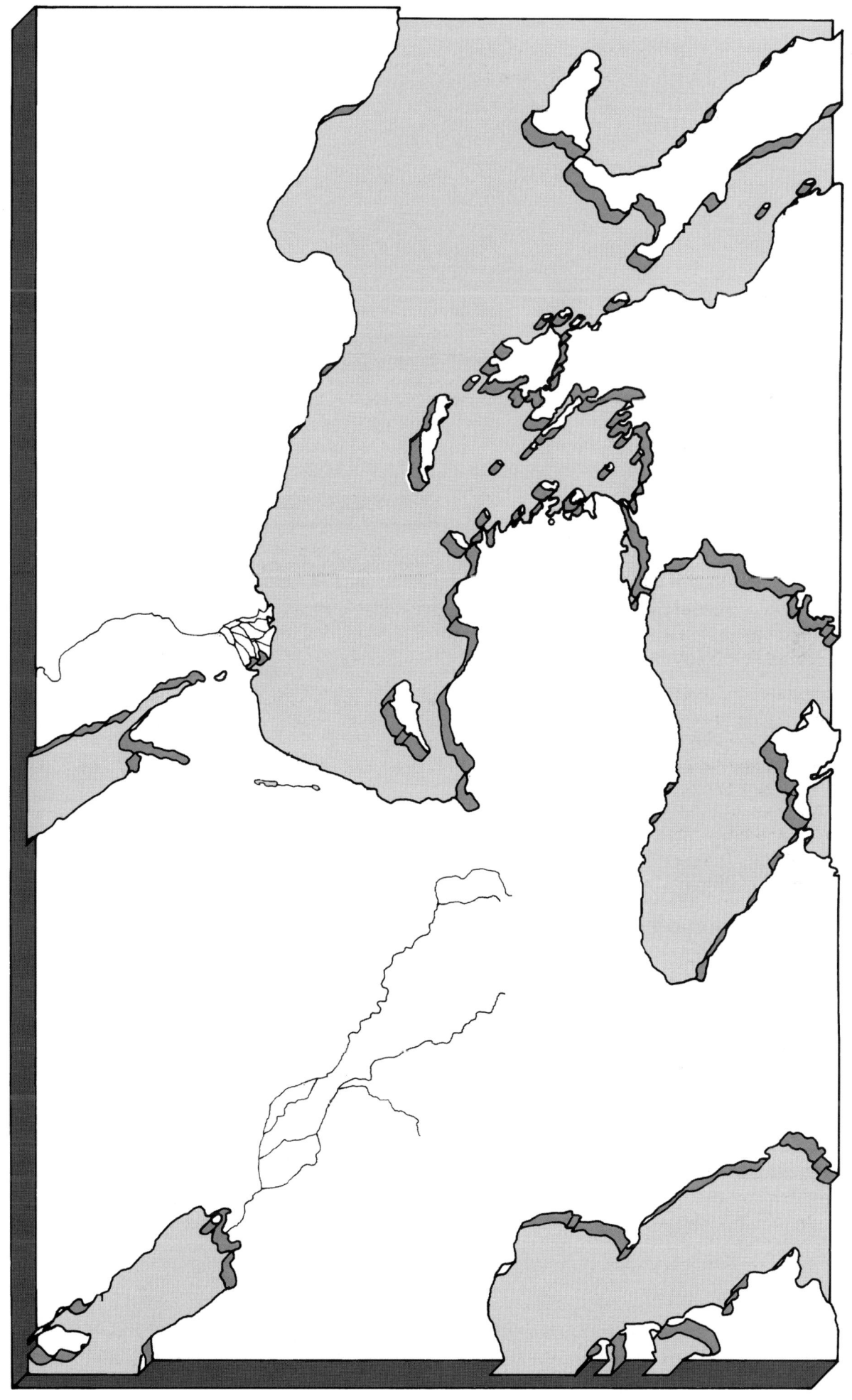

- Paul meets Lydia in Philippi—8.a and 16.a.
- In prison—8.b.
- Paul in Athens—8.b.
- Priscilla and Aquila—9.a; 16.a.
- A riot in Ephesus—9.a & b.
- Timothy and Titus—16.a.
- Trouble in Jerusalem—12.a & b.
- Shipwrecked—13.a & b.
- Paul in Rome—14.a & b.
- Paul's death—14.b.

2. Another group can research the modern names of the main areas named, using the atlas. Stress that you want to see where these are going before they put them on the map, again using thread to lead to the names around the edge.

3. Another group can plot the routes of the three journeys and of Paul's journey to Rome. They can draw these in four different colours on their practice maps and show them to you for checking before drawing them on the large map.

Further

Pupils could compile a souvenir book for Paul about his journeys, or write a diary for him.

Cross-references

- Ephesus—7.18.a & b
- Macedonia and Greece—7.19.a & b
- Rome—7.20.a & b.

Assembly suggestion

Introduce Paul's journeys and why he took them. Read what he said about them (page 110). Select some events and people to tell the others about, and pupils can then present what they have learned about these.

Others helped too

Community

Some other important people in Acts

NOTE: if all the work on Paul has been covered, some of these people will already have been studied. The pupils' work can be used again here if desired.

Introduction

Talk about the New Year's Honours list. What sort of people receive titles etc. in this? Point out that some people are honoured in this way for just doing their ordinary job for year after year, while others are honoured because they are famous. Any country or firm, or even school, has these two groups of people—those who just 'get on with the job' and those who are in the public eye.

Biblical or core material

Peter and Paul were important leaders of the church. But many other people worked hard, often in great danger, to help spread the news about Jesus.

Activity 1

Write pen-portraits of some or all of these people, using the references given. These can be displayed as an addition to the portraits of the disciples already done.
- Matthias—see page 104
- Philip—5.1.b; 5.3.b
- Lydia—5.8.a; 6.13.b
- Barnabas—5.6.a & b; 5.7.b; 5.8.a; 5.16.a
- Silas—5.8; 5.16.a
- Priscilla and Aquila—5.9.a; 5.16.a
- Andronicus and Junia—5.16.a
- Phoebe—5.16.a
- Timothy and Titus—5.8 (Timothy); 5.16.a; 6.1.b (Timothy); 6.14
- Luke—5.8; 5.16.a; 6.13.b; 9.5.b
- Mark—4.6; 5.8; 6.12, 6.13.a.

Activity 2

Design a special day for a church. Famous Christians, like Paul and Peter, already have their own special days in the church calendar. Choose one of the people in the list above: Priscilla and Aquila, Barnabas, Timothy, and Lydia would be good choices. Reread the information about your chosen person. How should their day be celebrated? What should be read at a service on that day? What could the members of the church do to remind them about the person? A booklet could be produced with instructions for the day. *Younger pupils* could design posters for a church for a special day about Lydia or Priscilla and Aquila, after being reminded about their story.

Further

Some pupils could begin to prepare the statements needed for the assembly—see below.

Assembly suggestion

Talk about the saying, 'Behind every great man there is…' In the early history of the church, one of the greatest men was Paul, but he could not have done what he did without the help and bravery of many other people. Label someone as Paul, and other people as some of the characters above. They can stand behind Paul as he tells the rest of the school about his achievements. Then they can emerge one at a time, and tell what they did to help Paul as he travelled and worked.

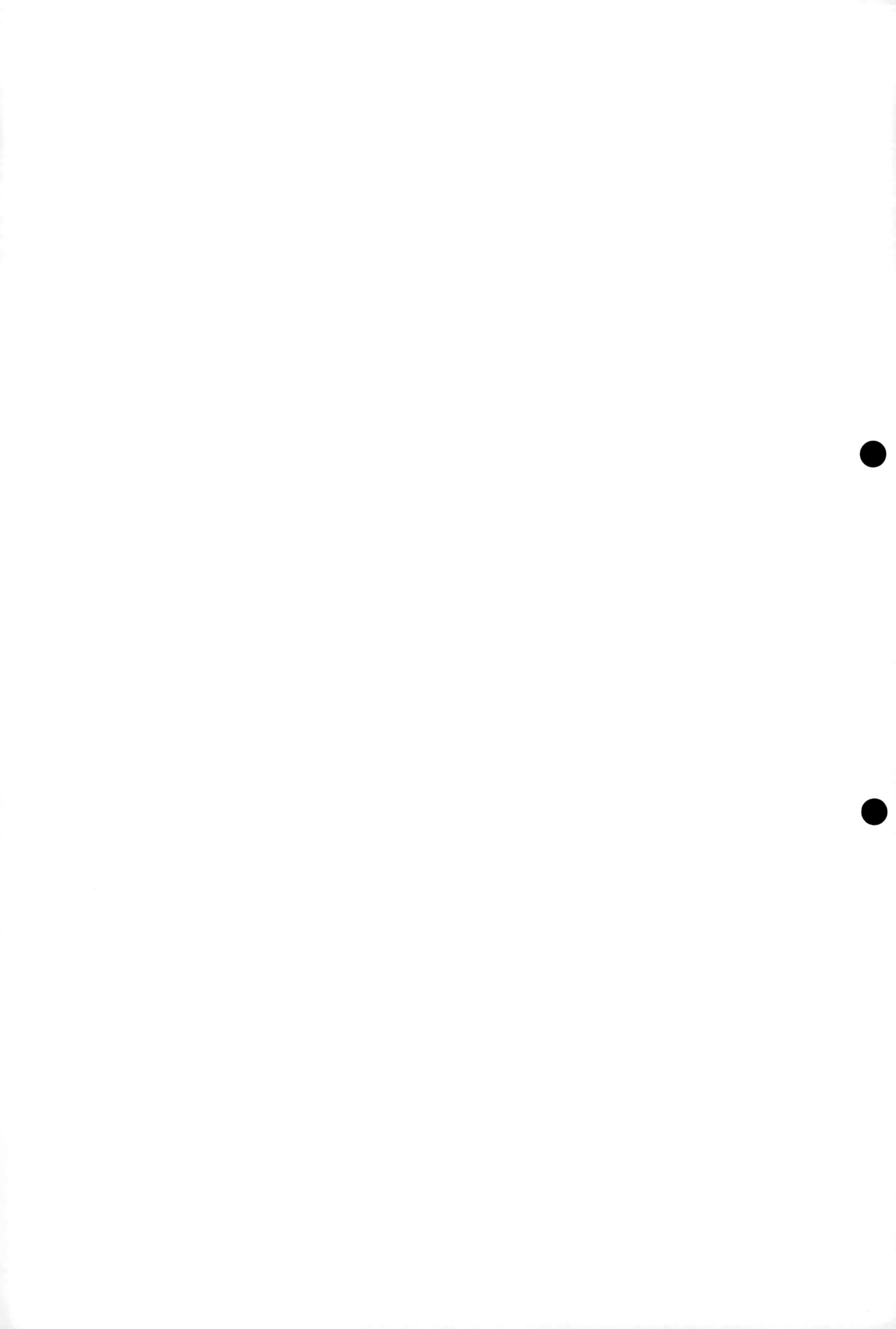

The Bible

A book of books

The Bible

NOTE: 'the Bible' is a huge subject, and few teachers are able to devote much lesson time to it. The lesson plans are divided into sections to try to make the choice of topics easier. If time allows, classes could study the introductory sections of 'What, why and how?' and 'A visit to the library' together, and then select from the activities that follow, individually or in groups.

What, why and how?

What is the Bible?
Ask this question, and comment on the answers. Discuss why each faith—or group of people who believe in the same things—needs a collection of their beliefs.

Read 6.1.a—all except 'The Jews and their Bible'—and 6.1.b—'The Christian New Testament'.

Bring out the two separate parts of the Bible and their importance. So the Bible is a collection of books, divided into two parts.

Activity 1

When someone writes a book, the first stage is often to send in a proposal—or a description of the book—to the publisher. Imagine that you want a publisher to publish a new edition of the Bible. The publisher has never heard of the Bible. Write a paragraph describing what the Bible is.

Younger pupils can fold a sheet of paper into two, as shown. On the cover, they can write and decorate the title 'The Bible'. On the left inside half, they can write 'The Old Testament', and write 'The New Testament' on the right side. On the back, they can write phrases—or complete sentences—about the two parts of the Bible.

Why do people still read the Bible?
The books of the Bible were written down many hundreds of years ago by many different people—the most recent are nearly two thousand years old! So why do people still read them? Christians believe that these writings were inspired by God and contain God's message—a message about God's love and care for people. This message is life-changing for many people.

Read 6.1.a—'The Jews and their Bible'.

Perhaps this could be tied in with work done on Judaism, pointing out the great respect the Jews have for their scriptures (the Old Testament). Reading and trying to follow them is still an integral part of their everyday lives for many Jews.

Read 6.1.b—'The Christians and their Bible' and 'Why read the scriptures?'

See what Paul said to the early Christians about the Jewish scriptures.

Read 6.19.a & b and 20.a & b.

Discuss reasons Christians might give for reading the Bible as you read these pages.

Activity 2

The publisher is interested in the proposal (see Activity 1), but isn't sure that anyone will buy it; surely no one wants to read such an old book? Write another paragraph giving some of the reasons Christians would give for reading this book. You could begin, 'Christians today still read the Bible. They believe that…'

Younger pupils could draw two or three heads of individual Christians, and write in speech bubbles the reasons these Christians would give for reading the Bible.

When and why was it written down?

NOTE: teachers can select appropriate material from this section.

How many kinds of story are there? One kind is history stories. Each culture and civilization has its own stories. Some are about their history. Some are myths and legends. People have always wanted to explain how the world works and to explain how people came to live here at all. They have made up stories called myths to try to answer these questions. Legends have grown up around the heroes of each country. Do they know any of the myths and legends of Rome and Greece? What about the legends of King Arthur? Many people now think that there was a warrior king in Britain who fought against invaders, and that the legends of King Arthur have grown up around his story.

 Read 6.2.a & b about some of the stories in the Bible.

Nowadays, we would write down a story that we wanted others to know, but what happened before people knew how to record things in writing? Talk about how stories were passed on orally. Do their own parents, grandparents, or other relatives tell them stories and rhymes? Have elder relatives ever told them stories about life in the Second World War? If they wanted to know about the battles and famous people in that war, where would they look to find the information? But ordinary people—like their relatives—can pass on family information about the war that would otherwise be lost when those people can no longer remember, or when they die. It was like this with the stories in the Bible.

Read 6.5.a about the stories in the Old Testament, and 6.12.a & b and 6.14.a about the New Testament.

Activity 1

Think about some of the reasons why the books of the Bible were written down. Write a paragraph as if you were the writer of one of the books explaining why you were now writing instead of passing on the information by telling it to people.

Younger pupils can play Chinese Whispers, passing a message round the class, and seeing if it becomes distorted. Talk about the need to pass on important information accurately, and relate this to the need to write down the stories and teachings of the Bible.

Further

Some pupils might like to look at the times when the books of the two testaments were collected together: Hebrew scriptures—6.9.a & b: Christian scriptures—6.15.a & b.

How was the Bible written down?

What languages was it in?
If you picked up a Bible today, what language would you expect it to be in? Was it written in this language at the beginning? Different parts of the Bible were written in different languages.

 Read 6.3.b—'Bible languages'.

As the message about Jesus spread around the world, more and more people wanted the Bible in their own language. For many years, books were handwritten and were too expensive for ordinary people to own. But when printing was invented, many more copies were available. The work of translation continues today. (See page 121)

Activity 1

Make larger copies of the Bible texts in Greek and Hebrew given here. Explain that these are the two main languages in which the Bible was written (the other was Aramaic). Mount them to make a wall-display appropriately labelled. Look up the text in a modern translation of the Bible (or in more than one), and copy thisature to add to the display.

ἐντολὴν καινὴν δίδωμι ὑμῖν, ἵνα ἀγαπᾶτε ἀλλήλους· καθὼς ἠγάπησα ὑμᾶς, ἵνα καὶ ὑμεῖς ἀγαπᾶτε ἀλλήλους.

John 13:34

ס כַּבֵּד אֶת־אָבִיךָ וְאֶת־אִמֶּךָ לְמַעַן יַאֲרִכוּן
יָמֶיךָ עַל הָאֲדָמָה אֲשֶׁר־יְהוָה אֱלֹהֶיךָ נֹתֵן לָךְ׃

Exodus 20:12

But how were the first Hebrew and the first Christian scriptures written?

Read 6.3.a & b.

Activity 2

The pupils can imitate some early methods of writing:
● clay: plasticene can be used. The end of a modelling tool could be the stylus.
● papyrus: some of today's handmade paper gives a good impression of what paper made from plant material can be like. The pupils could work on a small piece of this: or some of them might like to achieve similar results by making some recycled paper. Several kits for doing this are now available.
● vellum: orange peel can be dried in the sun and will then feel like leather. The pupils can experiment to find out whether it is more effective to write on it before drying or afterwards. Which gives the clearer result?

Alternatively, offcuts of leather are often available from local craftsmen, but pupils' moral preferences must be considered in their use.
● pottery: pieces of old pot washed up on the beach or found in the garden often have safe smooth edges. Alternatively, an air-drying modelling material, such as 'Modair', can be used. ('Modair' is available from Specialist Crafts Ltd. See the 'Useful addresses' section at the back of this book.)

What were the books like that were written in these ways?

Our books are usually like this one—discuss how the pages are held together, and how it is read.

Read 6.3.b—'Did you know?'

This talks about the origin of this type of book. Before this, books would be in the form of scrolls. Illustrate this with a sheet of paper.

Activity 3

The orange-peel used above cannot be rolled into a scroll as the original vellum was! But the pupils could copy a section of a Psalm (e.g. short excerpts 10.13.b) onto a sheet of paper, which they can treat with tea to give the appearance of old leather or parchment—see below. The paper can be rolled round a safe, smooth garden cane, such as bamboo.

Ageing paper
1. Crumple the piece of paper and then roughly smooth out.
2. Moisten a teabag, and drag across whole surface of paper.
3. Leave the paper to dry.
4. Pupils can then tear the edge of the paper to make it look older.

Alternative suggestions for the writing, or for individual passages to be displayed with this work, could be either 6.4.b—the quotation under 'Laws to light the way', prefaced with the words, 'The Bible says,' or 6.1.b—the quotation under 'Why read the scriptures?', prefaced with the words, 'Christians believe'.

Cross-references

● Writing—9.7.b.

A visit to the library

Talk about visiting the library. Are all the books in a library the same sort of book? How do the pupils know where to find the sort of book they need? Talk about the different categories of books in a library.

Activity 1

Make a list of these categories on the board. Include history, geography, stories, biographies, collections of letters, D.I.Y. books, music, poetry, encyclopedia, cookery books, handicrafts, petcare, humour.

Read out the following titles, asking the pupils in which category they would find each book. (This could be done orally, or in groups, with a 'scribe' in each one.)
● *How to fix that dripping tap*
● *Letters to my dog*
● *The Sahara Desert*
● *Every Child's Book of Facts*
● *Cooking Dinner—and other poems*
● *The Keyboard: how to deafen your parents without really trying*
● *The Best Teacher Jokes ever Written*
● *The Murderous Middle Ages*.

Go through the list: point out that sometimes it is obvious in which category books belong. Other books need more thought. The title can mislead!
The Bible is like a library. There are many different types of writing in it. Below are the main categories of writing in the Bible.

Class Activity 2

Make some 'books' for a wall display entitled 'The Library of the Bible'. Fold a sheet of paper in order to give a front and back cover and a spine—see diagram. A narrow strip of stiff card can be glued along the spine.

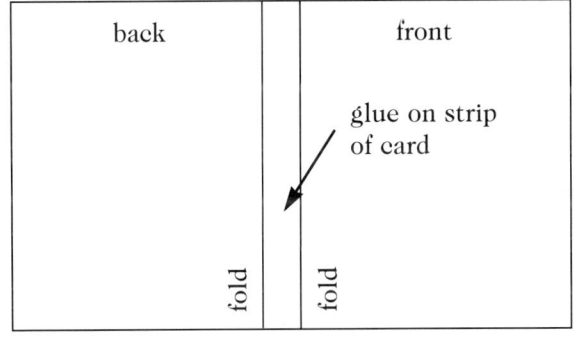

Pupils can:
- **either:** think about each briefly, and then write the type of writing on the spine of the book and a description of the type of writing and the names of one or two books within each category on the inside of the book:
- **or:** different groups can look at and write about each category. Some groups may prefer to illustrate the type of writing on each cover.

Further suggested activities are given for some categories of books. If preferred, the whole class can just work on one or two of these categories, depending on age, ability and the time available.

The Law

 Read 6.4.a & b.

Talk about the stories in these books—4.a. Relate the laws to the section on the Ten Commandments if this has been covered. The material there on the necessity of laws could be included here.

Activity 1

Pupils could make a phylactery to emphasize the importance of these books to Jews. (It may be possible to borrow a phylactery from a local resource centre: Articles of Faith, Bury Business Centre, Kay Street, Bury, Lanc., BL9 6BU could also provide them.)

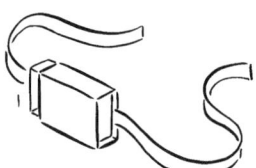

There is information about phylacteries in 9.20.a & b. Offcuts of leather could be used—see above. Suitable coloured material could be substituted. One possible method would be to cover a matchbox, and write appropriate verses on tiny scrolls of paper inside. A ribbon could then be threaded through the box as shown.

History

 Read 6.5.a & b. This covers the history books in the Old Testament.

Read 6.12.a & b and 13.a & b for the history books of the New Testament.

Discuss why the people needed to write down their history.

Activity 1

Pupils could look at examples of the times when other people's records confirm the information in the Bible: 2.1.b; 2.5.a; 3.9.a; 4.18.a; 10.1; 10.2; 10.3.

Prophecy

Read 6.6.a & b and 9.10.a & b.

Prophecy has several strands, including advice to the people and their rulers in particular, as well as telling what will happen in the future. It is this latter aspect that pupils may find difficult to understand. It may be helpful to talk about modern 'fortune tellers' and astrologers: even young children's magazines have a 'stars' page. Christians believe that, unlike these people, God's prophets had received their messages from God, and that the messages were accurate and came to fulfilment. Pupils could look at some of the messages about the Messiah and at the way Christians believe these were fulfilled at the birth of Jesus: page 55.

Poetry

Read 6.7.a & b.

Pupils can look at the different kinds of poetry in the Bible. Refer them to one of its oldest pieces of poetry, the Song of Deborah—page 38.

Activity 1

Pupils can write their own poetry in the style of Hebrew poetry. Explain the 'Patterns of Hebrew poetry' to them—6.7.a. Simple examples can be made up to provide a pattern for them. For example:
   *The window in the classroom is shattered;
   its glass is broken into thousands of pieces.*
and : *Today the sun is shining brightly;
   Darkness no longer rules the sky.*

Activity 2

This idea can be expanded into writing their own 'psalms' about the environment. (Some possible praise psalms to use as examples are: psalm 19:1–4; parts of psalm 136; psalm 148: psalm 150.) These could be written just as a celebration of nature. Or, if they wish, they can include gratitude to God for nature.

Wisdom writing

Few pupils will have met any 'wisdom writing'! Refer to page 48, discussing what the biblical idea of 'wisdom' is. Talk about our proverbs, and discuss the meaning of a few.

Read 6.8.a.

With *younger pupils*, it would be easier to concentrate on the book of Proverbs, and not to deal with the book of Job. (Two possible activities are on page 49.)

Activity 3

A display of the work from either or both of these activities could be made. They could *either* make their own book of proverbs, *or* they could draw/cut out silhouettes of each other, using black paper, a torch and a screen or white wall. The proverbs could then be added in speech bubbles. Could they produce a silhouette of a man's head for Solomon to show some of his proverbs?

Letters

Read 6.14.a & b (not Revelation).

Discuss why people wrote these letters. The danger of the times in which they were written is described in 5.15.a & b; other difficulties the writers faced are described in 5.18.a & b. (There is more information about the letters in 5.11 and 5.17.)

Activity 1

Pupils can write a letter as if they were one of the writers of the letters in the New Testament. They have been asked why they keep on writing letters to people. They are to explain why they feel it is important to do so. The letters can be written on miniature scrolls. The letters could be written in modern letter form if practice in this is needed. Or the pupils can look at the differences between our letter-writing conventions and those of Paul's time. 5.11.a gives the typical Epistle's arrangement.

How did we get our Bible?

The history of the translation and availability of the Bible is a huge subject! One way of tackling it would be to draw a simple timeline (from 1 CE to 2000 CE) which could then be fastened along a wall. The pupils can then work out the position of some of the important events on this line. The relative importance of each could be discussed by pupils as they work. These can be marked with simple arrows and a sentence describing the event and its importance. This information could be expanded if more time was to be spent on the subject. Below are some of the main highlights in the long history of the Bible as a book.

Timeline
- 'Gathering the books together'—6.9.a & b
- 'The Greek translation'—6.10.a & b
- 'The Deuterocanonical books'—6.11.a & b
- 'The Christian Bible'—6.15.a & b
- 'Order of importance'—6.15.b
- 'Many languages'—6.16.a & b
- 'Illuminated manuscripts'—6.16.a
- 'Retelling the Bible'—6.17.a & b
- 'Books for all'—6.18.a & b: 'Printing'—a; 'The Reformation'—a; Translations—b; 'Did you know?'—the Bible divided into chapters and verses—b
- 'The Scrolls by the Dead Sea'—6.9.b.

Assembly suggestion

Pupils can present some of the information they have gathered about the Bible.

Other suggested topics for study

One approach to using the books as a source of information on a chosen topic is given on page 8 of the *Bible World Factfinder*. This shows how to find out more about a specific character.

Another approach is described on page 10 of the same book. This shows how to research a particular topic.

Below are a few ideas for further research, on some topics which some pupils might wish to look into for themselves. Basic references are given, but these are not exhaustive. Very often, the topics are easily identified by the chapter headings themselves, and any further information needed can be found using the indices.

Places of worship
(This could tie in with work done on places of worship today.)
- 9.2
- 9.11
- 9.3—Priests and Levites
- Factfinder—frontispiece—Herod's temple
- Index—'synagogues'.

Children's lives
- 8.6.a.—children's rhyme
- 8.7 and 8.8—festivals
- 8.11—a new baby
- 8.12—growing up, work and school
- 8.13—fun and games.

Eating!
- 8.14—food
- 8.15—cooking
- 8.16—meals.

Living in biblical times
Life in an ordinary home
- 8.19.a—hygiene
- 8.4—the home
- 8.12—growing up
- 8.14, 8.15 and 8.16—cooking and food
- 8.18—clothes
- 8.6—farming.

Life in a richer home
- 8.19.b—hygiene
- 8.5—the home
- 8.12—growing up
- 8.14, 8.15 and 8.16—cooking and food
- 8.18.b—clothes.

Other areas of family life
- 8.7–8.12.

Timeline

Some pupils might like to draw a timeline for the classroom wall. They can use those on pages 22 and 23 of the *Factfinder*, and the categories in 9.1. They could colour code these rough time periods, and then insert the names of any biblical characters and events they study as the time goes by.

CHRONOLOGICAL INDEX

OLD TESTAMENT

Creation	10
The Fall	28
The Flood	12
Abraham	30
Jacob and Esau	32
Joseph (1)	34
Joseph (2)	14
Moses	16
The Ten Commandments	18
The Covenant	21
Joshua	36
Judges—Deborah and Gideon	38
Ruth	41
Samuel and Saul	43
David and Goliath	46
Solomon	48
Elijah	22
The Exile and the three friends	50
Esther	52
Jonah	23

NEW TESTAMENT

John the Baptist	56
Jesus' birth	58
Jesus' baptism	62
Jesus' temptation	64
The disciples	65
Jesus' miracles	67
Jesus' teaching	74, 79
People Jesus met	71
The entry into Jerusalem	82
Jesus in the Temple	84
The Last Supper	86
The arrest	88
The death of Jesus	90
The Resurrection of Jesus	92, 94
The Ascension	96
Pentecost	98
The Holy Spirit	97–102
The early church and Stephen	104
Peter	106
Paul	108
Paul's missionary journeys	110
Other people in Acts	113
The Bible	116
Other topics for study	123

PEOPLE INDEX

A
Abraham	30
Adam and Eve	28
Andrew—see under Disciples	
Andronicus and Junia	113

B
Barnabas	110, 113
Bartholomew—see under Disciples	

D
Daniel	51
David	46, 120
Deborah	38
Disciples	65, 66, 104

E
Elijah	22
Esau	32
Esther	52

G
Gideon	38
God—main section	9–25
Goliath	46
Good Samaritan	72, 79

H
Holy Spirit—main section	97–102

J
Jacob	32
Jairus	70
James	65, 66, 104
James the Lesser—see under Disciples	
Jesus—main section	55–96
Joanna	72
John	65, 66, 70, 90, 106, 117
John the Baptist	56, 62
Jonah	23
Joseph	14, 34
Joseph, Mary's husband	58
Joseph of Arimathea	90
Joshua	36
Judas	88, 105
Judges	38

L
Luke	110, 113, 117
Lydia	112, 113

M
Mark	113, 117
Mary Magdalene	72, 92
Mary, mother of Jesus	58, 72
Mary and Martha	72
Matthew	65, 66, 72, 117
Moses	16, 18

N	
Nicodemus	90
Noah	12
P	
Paul	108, 110
Peter	65, 66, 70, 88, 94, 106
Philip—see under Disciples	
Philip and the Ethiopian	104
Phoebe	113
Priscilla and Aquila	112, 113
R	
Rahab	36
Ruth	41
S	
Samuel	43
Saul	43
Silas	113
Simon—see Peter	
Simon the Zealot—see under Disciples	
Solomon	22, 48
Stephen	104
Suzanna	72
T	
Thaddaeus—see under Disciples	
Thomas	65, 66, 94
Timothy and Titus	112, 113
Z	
Zacchaeus	72

THEMATIC INDEX

This is intended as a guide to themes and topics which feature on R.E. syllabi throughout the country and which are found in this book. It is not an exhaustive list of such topics and themes.

A	
Accepting and valuing others	71
Advent	56, 58
Anger	84
B	
Baptism	56, 62
Bible	116–122
Birth	58
Bravery	30, 36, 38, 46, 50, 52, 104, 106, 108, 113
C	
Caring for others	18, 41, 79
Caring for the environment	10, 13
Change	108
Children	43, 72
Choices	23, 28, 43, 52, 64
Church	98, 104
Community	104, 113
Creation	10
D	
Decisions—see Choices	
Defending others	52, 84
Dishonesty	32
Disobedience	23, 28
Doubt	94
E	
Early church	98, 103–113
Early writing	117
Encouragement	108
Environment	10
Epistles	121
F	
Failure	23, 28, 32, 34, 43, 48, 94, 106
Fairness	18, 34, 41
Family life	14, 32, 34, 41
Favouritism	34
Fear	38, 88
Feelings	88, 92
Forgiveness	14, 32, 46, 77, 79, 94
Free will	28
Friends	41, 65, 71, 113
G	
Gifts and giving	58
Gifts of the Holy Spirit	96, 100
God—	
cares	16, 22
Creator	10

is in control	14
is trustworthy	12
Lawgiver	18
loves	10, 12, 14, 16, 21, 22, 23, 46, 58, 67, 71, 90
just	22
merciful	23
patient	38
powerful	22
Provider	16
Rescuer	16, 38, 46, 90
surprising choices	43, 46
Growth	104

H

Holy Spirit—	
gifts of the	100
Helper	102
in the Bible	102
Jesus' teaching about the	96, 98
Symbols of the	98, 102

J

Jealousy	32, 34
Jesus'—	
care for people	67, 71
Kingship	58, 82, 96
life	55–96
love	62, 67, 71, 86, 90
parables	79
power	67
teaching about—God	76
—Kingdom of God	77
—prayer	76
—self	74
titles	58
Joy	67, 70, 92, 94

L

Law	18, 120
Letters	121
Love	41, 67, 88, 90, 91

M

Making things	10
Martyrs	65, 104
Meals—special	16, 86

N

Neighbours	41, 72, 79

O

Obedience	28, 30, 36, 38
Overcoming fears	50, 88, 90

P

Parables	74, 79
Passover	16, 86
Pentecost	98
Perseverance	30
Poetry	38, 121
Preparing for Jesus	56, 58
Promises -	12, 30, 41
and covenants	21
of the Holy Spirit	96, 98
Prophecy	120
Proverbs	48, 121

R

Responsibility to others	18, 23, 62
Rules	18

S

Sadness	28, 70, 86, 90
Setting an example	23
Standing up for what is right	46, 50, 64
Success	36, 106
Surprises	92
Symbols	98, 102

T

Teamwork	41, 113
Telling the truth	18
Temper	84
Trust	12, 21, 30, 36, 38, 65

V

Value of children—see under Children	
Value of the individual	71

W

Wisdom	48
Wisdom writing	48, 121

Useful addresses

Action Aid, Freepost BS4868, Chard, Somerset, TA20 1BR (includes child sponsorship schemes)

Articles of Faith, Bury Business Centre, Kay Street, Bury, Lanc., BL9 6BU

CAFOD, Romero Close, Stockwell Road, London, SW9 9TY

Christian Aid, P.O. Box 100, London, SE1 7RT

Friends of the Earth, 26 Underwood Street, London, N1 7JQ

Operation Christmas Child (Samaritan's Purse), P.O. Box 732, Wrexham, Clwyd, LL13 9ZA. (Tel. 0701 0702999) (the 'shoebox' appeal)

Oxfam, 274, Banbury Road, Oxford, OX2 7DZ

TEAR FUND, 100, Church Road, Teddington, Middlesex, TW11 8QE

The Toybox Charity, P.O. Box 660, Amersham, Buckinghamshire, HP6 6EA (working with the street children of Guatemala)

Specialist Crafts Ltd., P.O. Box 247, Leicester, LE1 9QS.

Young Ornithologists' Club, R.S.P.B., Dept. 1664, The Lodge, Sandy, Beds., SG19 2DL.

Local homes for the homeless often run appeals for canned food, toiletries, etc.